BUDBURY

From hillfort to houses

Pamela Slocombe
and Roy Canham

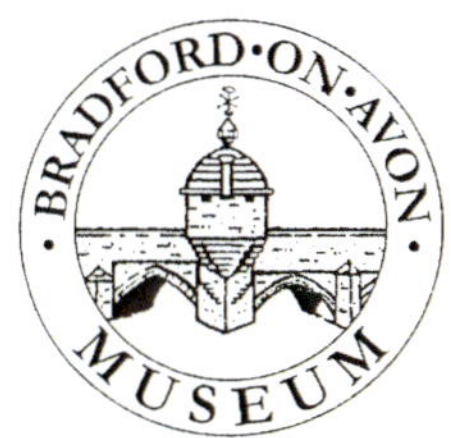

Ex Libris Press in association with Bradford-on-Avon Museum

Published in 2019 by
Ex Libris Press
11 Regents Place
Bradford-on-Avon
Wiltshire   BA15 1ED
www.ex-librisbooks.co.uk

in association with Bradford-on-Avon Museum
www.bradfordonavonmuseum.co.uk

ISBN 978-1-912020-74-4

Origination by Ex Libris Press
Bradford-on-Avon

Typeset in 10.5/14 point Souvenir

Printed by TPM Ltd.
Farrington Gurney, Somerset

CONTENTS

Introduction

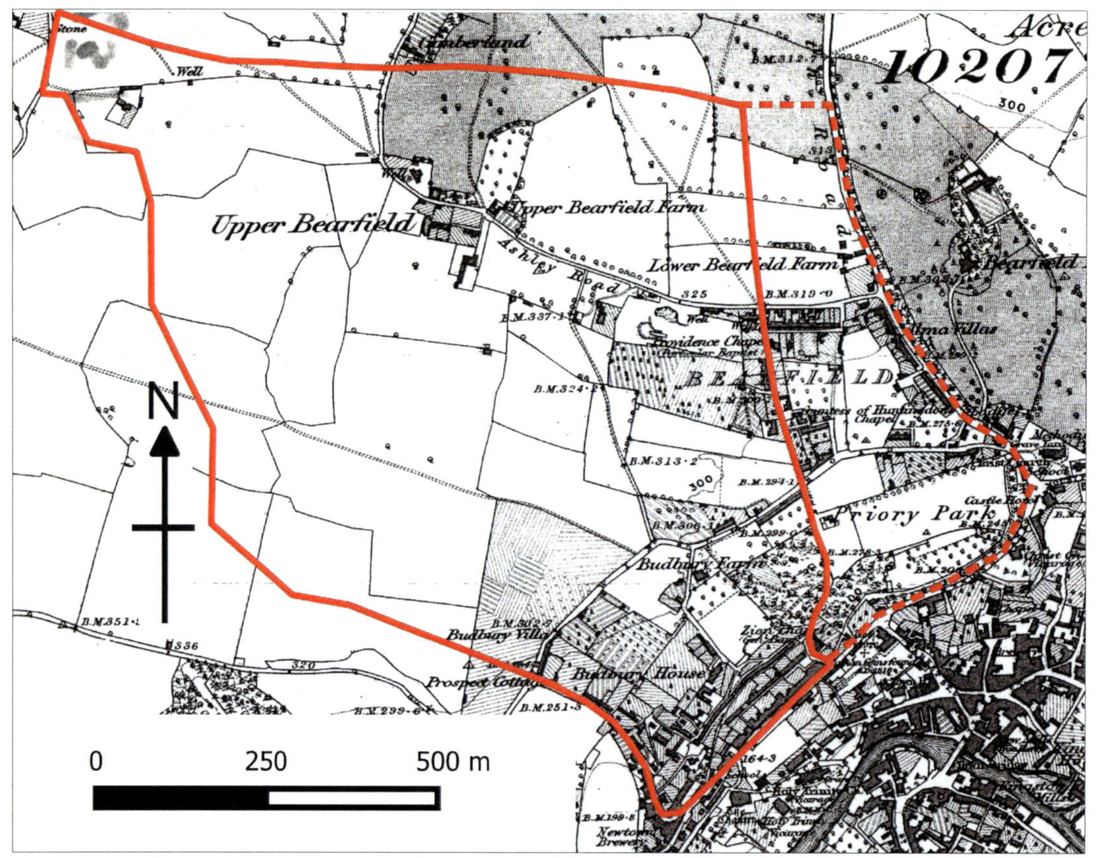

Fig. 1:   Budbury study area

Introduction

Today people think of Budbury as just the top of the hill overlooking Bradford-on-Avon, although there is a road called Budbury Tyning on the north side of Winsley Road. Historically, however, Budbury covered a much larger area and was an estate of some importance at different periods.

Originally it was bounded on the south side by Newtown. On the north it merged into Bearfield. The western boundary was Palmer's Lane (now Wine Street) with some lands in Hare Knapp beyond. From the top of Palmer's Lane, Budbury field names indicate that it extended to the edge of the Great Ashley estate. On the east, if it followed the boundary of Winsley tithing, it was bounded by the lane called Conigre Hill with its continuation, Huntingdon Street. However, the topography suggests that at some earlier stage in its history, perhaps Anglo-Saxon, it might have stretched to Masons Lane (fig.1). Bearfield and Hare Knapp were common open fields in which Budbury had isolated strips of land. These fields were progressively enclosed from the 16th century if not before.

The Anglo-Saxon administrative system divided the country into Hundreds which, in turn, were sub-divided into tithings. Budbury was within the hundred of Bradford and mostly in the tithing of Winsley. The west part of Bearfield common field was in Winsley tithing but the east part was in Leigh and Woolley except for one strip of land immediately east of Huntingdon Street which was in Trowle tithing and another strip which was part of Bradford borough. These detached portions were caused by farms in the other tithings historically having land there. Hare Knapp was completely in Winsley tithing. It was not until just before 1800 that the area of the hillfort itself was added to Bradford borough tithing instead of Winsley.[1]

Taking the present Budbury with its former lands beyond St Laurence School towards Great Ashley raises the possibility that the medieval estate could have been a continuation of that of the Roman villa in the grounds of the school. Perhaps we could go further and see the area as an Iron Age estate taken over by the Romans. There is still much that is unsure and it is hoped that this account will provide a starting point for further research.

1   The Archaeology of Budbury

Prehistory

The study area (fig.1) is part of a limestone plateau flanking the River Avon between Bradford on Avon and Winsley. An extension to this zone, stretching from Budbury to Inwood at Monkton Farleigh was the subject of a recent archaeological study based on an airborne Lidar survey.[1] The project revealed that the whole area contains the remains of ancient field systems originating in the middle to late Bronze Age, i.e. from around 1200BC.

The banks or lynchets that define these fields are also preserved as low-profile earthworks in fields at the very edge of the built-up area, and can be seen in the Lidar image of pastures adjacent to Ashley Road and Bath Road (fig.2). These features form a complex pattern, evidently derived from a long period of agricultural use, much of it prehistoric and Roman but also including field boundaries shown on the tithe map of 1841. The important point is that this type of early land use would have continued across the Budbury area to the very top of the limestone scarp overlooking the town.

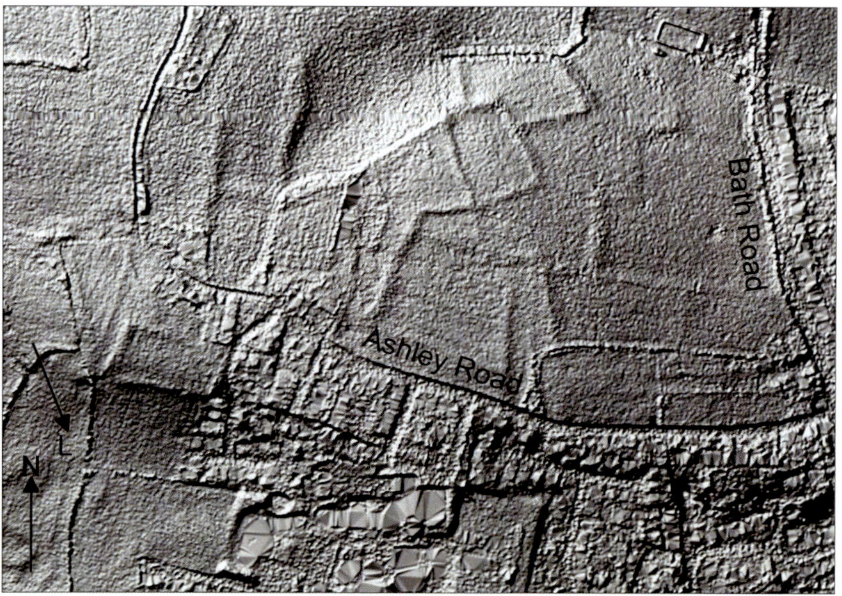

Fig, 2: Ancient field-systems revealed by Lidar survey north of Ashley Road

In this vast zone of prehistoric and Romano-British farming, there is only one known settlement contemporary with the field systems, located on land belonging to Church Farm north of Winsley.[2] As we turn our attention to evidence from Budbury itself the indications are that the necessary settlement evidence is to be found here, on land overlooking the Avon, with access to resources the river might provide. As we shall see, these settlements range from the Bronze Age to the Roman period, established to farm the vast plateau hinterland of early fields shown by the Lidar survey.

A hint of this ancient landscape appears in an account published by Rev. W. H. Jones.[3] He refers to 'traces of earthworks in fields on the promontory, since levelled and built over.' This reference is intriguing, firstly in suggesting that the evidence of ancient landscape features as seen adjacent to Ashley Road did indeed extend across Budbury and secondly that these features suffered the same fate as almost all the field-system banks mapped in the Lidar survey. An explanation for this may be found two miles to the west at Inwood. Here the banks or 'lynchets' enclosing each prehistoric field are well preserved. They are in fact stone walls, totally different to the Wessex chalkland lynchets which vanish rapidly under Medieval and modern ploughing. These stone obstacles were no doubt cleared at some date to facilitate better use of the land, and in Budbury another factor was building development.

The clearest indication of prehistoric settlement in Budbury came in 1969 when part of the Scheduled Ancient Monument was threatened with destruction. At that time such features were not sacrosanct. An owner simply needed to give three months notice of planned development to the then Ministry of Public Building and Works, and the latter organisation would arrange rescue excavation prior to destruction.

The development site was located on land bounded by Winsley Road on the north and Budbury Place on the east. A Bradford on Avon councillor named Guy Underwood had noticed a circular mound here, and carried out an excavation which revealed curving ditches adjacent to the mound. He concluded that this was a burial mound and succeeded in getting it Scheduled. The 1969 rescue excavation was carried out by Dr Geoffrey Wainwright,[4] later to become Chief Inspector of Ancient Monuments at English Heritage. The results were remarkably informative. The circular mound was in fact the corner of a defensive bank, flanked by two ditches (fig. 3). A considerable quantity of Early Iron Age pottery came to light, mostly of types dating from the very beginning of the Iron Age, c700-600BC. Wainwright had no difficulty in concluding that he

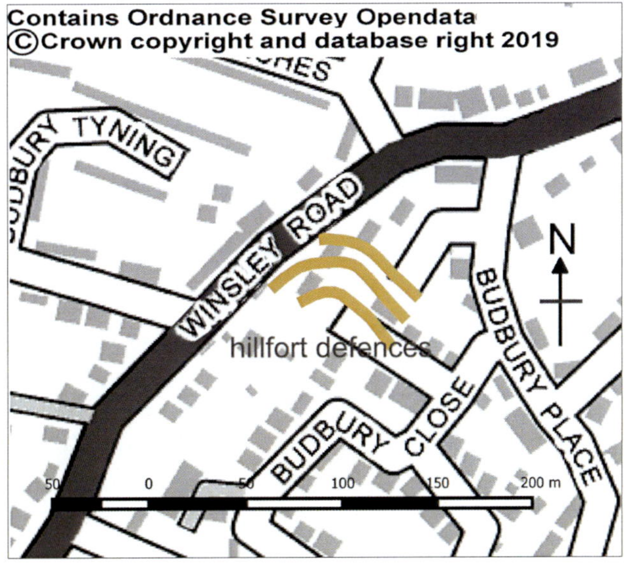

Fig. 3: Plan of corner of Iron Age hillfort

had discovered the corner of an Iron Age hillfort. A problem facing him was determining the overall layout of the site. He commissioned a topographic survey of the area and the resultant contour mapping indicated that the hillfort was of the well-known promontory type, perhaps best known at Crickley Hill in Gloucestershire. Neither Wainwright nor any previous author had discussed the possible implications of the 'bury' element of the place-name, so commonly an indication of an Iron Age fortification – local examples are Battlesbury and Scatchbury, two huge hillforts near Warminster. Another debate notable for its absence concerns the fate of the Budbury hillfort defences over the millennia. These huge structures are not readily demolished – the single instance known to the author is the levelling of Chisenbury Trundle to make way for Upavon airfield in WWII. Wainwright suggested that 'buildings, roads and gardens' had removed it, but the levelling was so extensive that some other cause seems likely. His excavations revealed that the inner element of the defences was a stone rampart, in effect an enormous wall some 5m wide, and this certainly would have attracted stone robbers down the ages, first for the Roman villa found at St Laurence School, secondly for later buildings of the town below.

What is surprising is that such activities should have levelled these prehistoric defences so thoroughly. Budbury was substantially undeveloped until the 1970s, yet not a vestige of any bank or ditch appears on Ordnance Survey maps – OS land surveyors were astute in the recording of surviving monuments and noted such features in the OS archive. The only instances we have of extant archaeological features are the observations of Jones and Underwood noted above, and a remarkable sketch made by the Rev. John Skinner in 1819 which shows a ditch which he describes as part of 'The British Settlement above Bradford' (fig. 4).

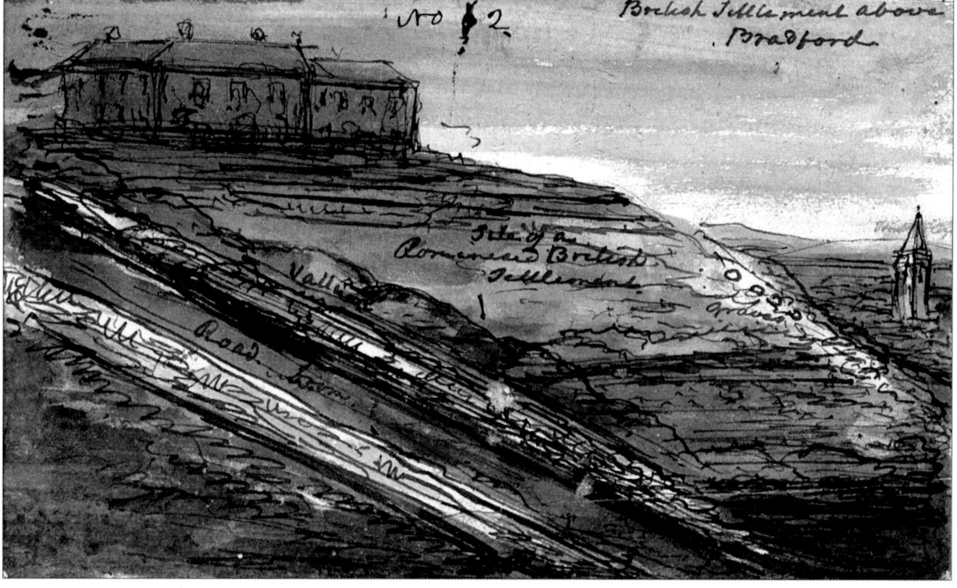

Fig. 4: Sketch of 'British Settlement' by Skinner (BL)

There is perhaps another possibility. M. and H. Whittock have suggested that during the reign of Cnut other Anglo-Saxon period stone wall defences were razed, comparable sites being Daws Castle (Somerset), Cricklade (Wiltshire) and Christchurch (Dorset).[5] They suggest that the motivation might have been to remove fortresses associated with Cnut's predecessor Aethelred II which might have continued to provide focal points for resistance to the new regime after Cnut's accession in 1016.

Although the 1969 excavation was focussed on the hillfort defences, some occupation evidence came to light. The postholes of a rectangular hut, some 6.5 x 4.25m, were uncovered just 5m from the inner face of the rampart.[6] This situation echoes the layout at Maiden Castle in Dorset where the hillfort huts were clustered along the rampart inner edge. A mass of Iron Age pottery and numerous small finds were found on the Budbury hut-site, including objects of iron comprising a knife, a clamp and a possible plough-share tip. Spindle whorls, part of a clay loom weight and clay sling missiles were also found. The gardens of houses throughout Budbury Close are likely to be rich in Early Iron Age archaeology as the 1969 hut features were a mere 50cm beneath the surface.

Discoveries made during the development of Budbury Ridge in 1986, together with excavations at Budbury Manor and the Skinner sketch, have allowed a fresh projection of the hillfort layout (fig. 5).[6] There is also some likelihood that Budbury saw human occupation before the Early Iron Age. The watching brief at Budbury Ridge recorded numerous ditches which do not appear to relate to the hillfort, and an Early Iron Age pit found near the southern end of Budbury Close had been dug into the filling of an earlier ditch.[7] These are hints therefore of Bronze Age activity, not uncommon on hillfort locations.

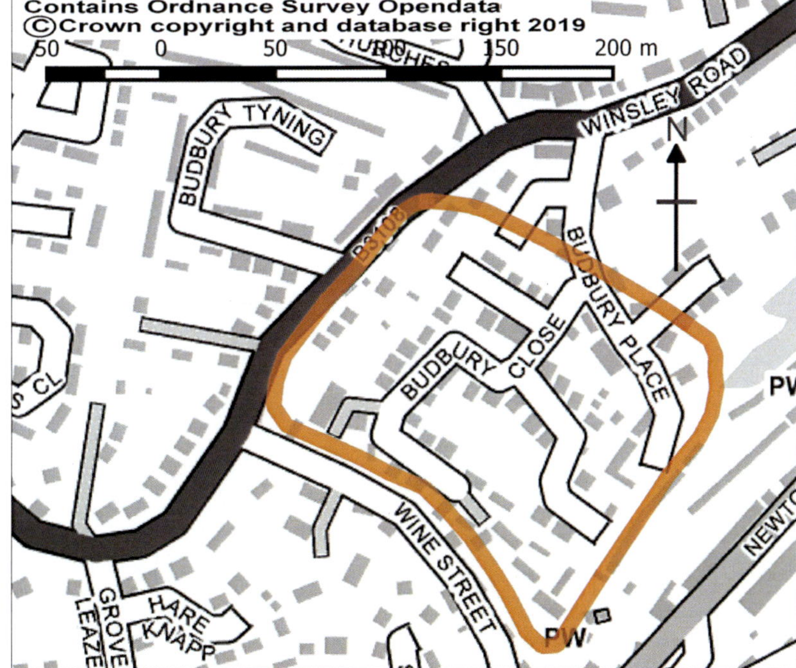

Fig. 5: Possible layout of the Budbury Iron Age hillfort

The Roman period (AD43–410)

The existence of a Roman settlement at Budbury was suggested by W. H. Jones in 1859, referring to the discovery there of a large number of Roman coins. The Skinner sketch of c1820 contains a note indicating a Roman settlement, apparently within the hillfort enclosure. The 1969 hillfort excavation revealed Romano-British sherds in the upper levels of the inner ditch, and the same excavation yielded coins and coarse pottery of late 3rd–4th century date. Further evidence has come to light in the form of four Roman stone coffins or 'sarcophagi', found scattered across the area (fig. 6).This is an odd distribution in that Roman burials tend to come in cemeteries. Stone coffins by their nature attract attention so it is uncertain whether any one of these represented a Roman cemetery.

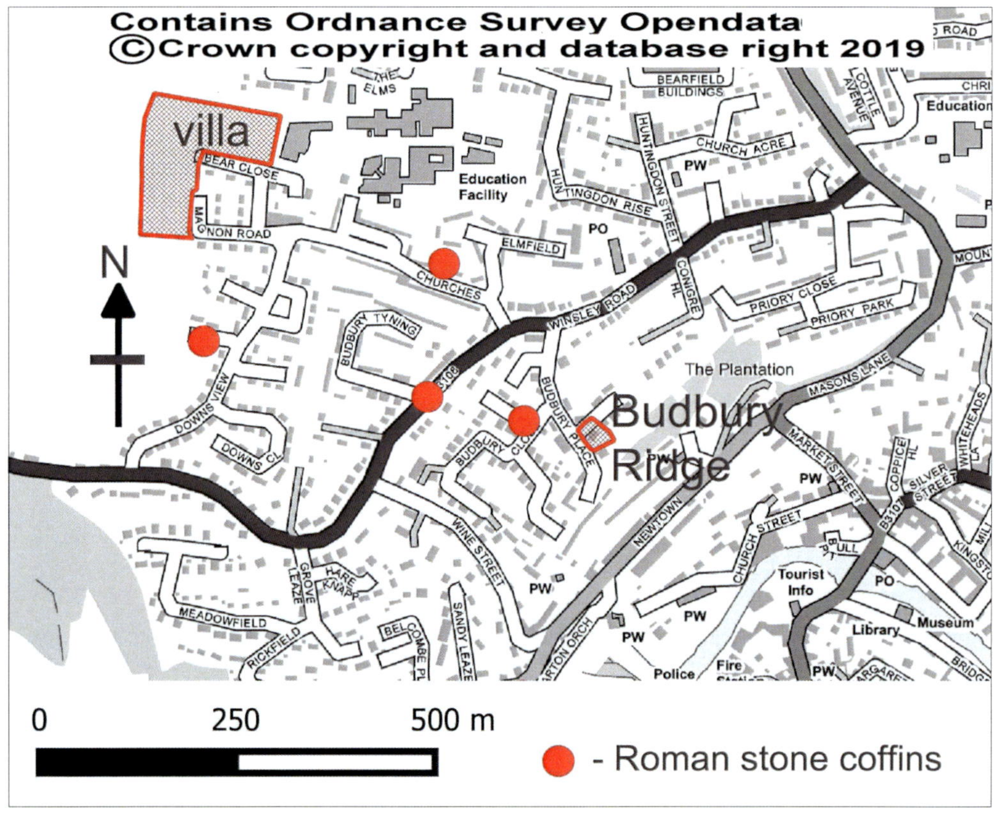

Fig. 6: Roman Budbury

Clear evidence of Roman occupation emerged in 2000 with the discovery of a Roman villa in the grounds of St Laurence School (fig 6). While on the periphery of our study area, this site must surely offer some explanation for the Roman discoveries within Budbury itself. Villas are interpreted not as isolated farmsteads, but as the core of substantial estates. The background lies in the rationale behind the original Roman invasion of Britain in AD43 – to secure a territory that had a remarkable reputation for the production of grain. We know from Roman writers that this country was exporting grain to Europe long before the Roman conquest and without the benefit of the infrastructure which that event provided. The prehistoric field-systems that covered the Budbury hinterland were adopted by the new Roman owners and no doubt extended.

Aspects of this Roman villa design and history offer intriguing insights into life in Roman Budbury. One unique feature is the discovery that there were two buildings of identical plan, one of which is the villa proper, the other 'designed as a utilitarian working building behind a grand façade mirroring that of the main house'.[8] The estate management function is clearly evident. The second is the discovery of a baptistery inserted circa AD400 into the main dwelling, indicating the arrival of Christianity. The Romanised inhabitants of Budbury and the surrounding area were thus the precursors of those responsible for the ecclesiastical foundations of Bradford itself in the Saxon period.

Returning to the 1986 watching brief at Budbury Ridge, Roman occupation debris was found in some quantity, in an area marked by the black soil generated by such activity (fig. 6). The pottery fragments range through the Roman period, but the coins are concentrated on the years AD275–410. Of special interest was the discovery of a well-built stone wall. These finds were recorded during building work and interpretation is difficult. The site is located on a prominent location overlooking the river valley, and probably just within the south-east corner of the hillfort. Was this a farmstead forming part of the villa estate or was the well-built structure a Roman temple, similar to examples known from other hillforts?

In recent years members of the Museum Research Group have been given verbal reports of mosaic pavements observed in two separate locations in the Huntingdon Street and The Conigre area, intriguing discoveries worthy of further research. Thus on present evidence the nature and extent of Roman occupation in Budbury is difficult to assess, but it is certain that more will come to light.

Saxon and Medieval periods

Excavations carried out in the garden of Budbury Manor between 2009 and 2015[9] brought to light sherds of Medieval pottery from the filling of the hillfort inner ditch. This pottery, the earliest dating from soon after the Norman Conquest, is certain to have come from the manor house but was stratified in sand and rubble deposits used to backfill the ditch. A little to the north Wainwright in 1969 found a mass of Medieval sherds, mostly of 14th–15th century date. The fabric of the house dates from the 15th century but the history of Budbury manor suggests occupation of the site from the 11th century at least (see below). A remarkable group of glazed Medieval ridge tiles shows the high status of the building. Some 50m to the north-east, Budbury Farm was part of the medieval complex. On the opposite side of the former lane fronting the farm, excavations in the present garden of Budbury Farm also revealed Medieval sherds, possibly indicating further Medieval dwellings nearby.

Further south at Budbury Ridge a large quantity of post-Roman pottery was recovered during the 1986 building work. There were numerous small finds and the site plan indicates the location of a Medieval building but no details are given. The pottery range is broad, c.1200–1800, suggestive of continuous occupation throughout the Middle Ages and beyond.

In the context of Medieval settlement patterns, a place-name such as 'Budbury' implies the existence of a village or hamlet. The evidence we have runs from the Winsley road to the scarp top, probably outlining a small hamlet in which Budbury Place or its precursor was the main street. Historic maps show a lane or track which approached the area from the north (fig.7), and this may have been a route into Bradford on which the small Budbury settlement developed. Activity seen in the Budbury Manor excavations is relevant here. The deliberate filling of the main part of the hillfort inner ditch may indicate that the feature was in use as a hollow way. The surface was made more substantial when the section of ditch in front of the house was cobbled, probably at the time of a substantial re-build of the property in the 15th century. This places the house in a principal position at the northern end of the settlement, and the route south from the house is likely to have continued to use the prehistoric ditch, a little to the east of Budbury Place. Possibly the houses shown on 19th century maps on the west side of Budbury Place occupied Medieval sites.

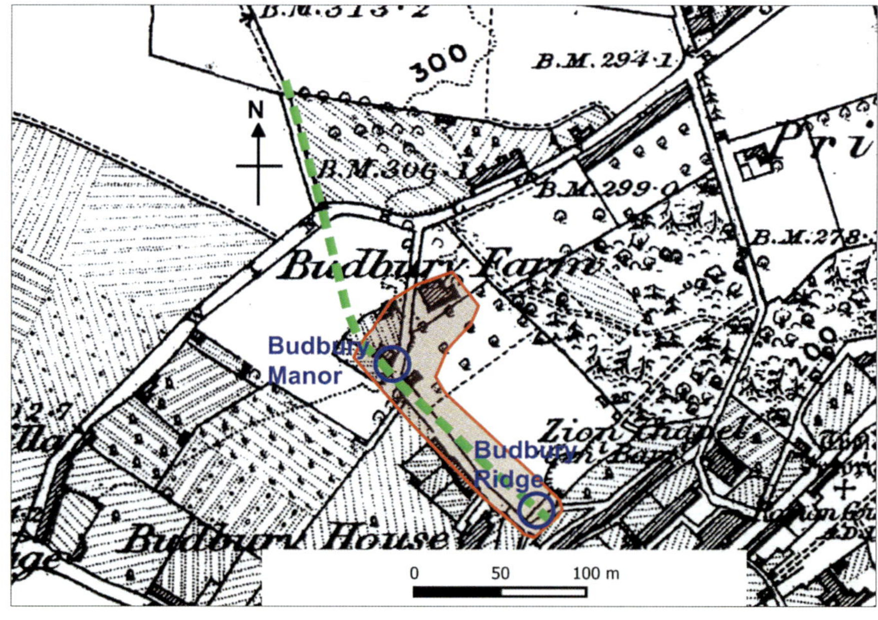

Fig. 7: Medieval Budbury

2   The Medieval Period

The hundred of Bradford was originally identical in extent with the royal manor of Bradford. Gradually some sections were granted away so that by 1001 Wingfield, Westwood and Monkton Farleigh and, by 1086, Budbury and Cumberwell were separately owned.

Budbury as a knight's fee

Many small sub-manors were created before the Norman Conquest, particularly in the 10th century. Landlords of large estates progressively enfeoffed (made freehold) areas within their manors, creating small holdings of up to a few hides. This was to reward their followers but principally to provide for the military service demanded by English kings.[1] The practice was also used by the king himself and this was probably the case at Budbury since it was held under the king in 1086. By 1070 even monasteries had to provide the king with knights. These small estates, carved out of larger units, were given new names, often combining a personal name and a suffix. Budbury is thought to have been named after an Anglo-Saxon thane called Budda, a 'well evidenced personal name' and 'burgh', meaning a fortress or fortified place.[2]

It may be unusual for a knight's fee to be created as close to the centre of a royal estate as Budbury is to the villa regalis, or royal residence, which is known to have been at Bradford. The explanation must be that the old hillfort by the river crossing was a place which required a permanent guard.

The process of becoming a knight as recorded in the Middle Ages was elaborate. A young man who was heir to a knight's fee first became a squire (shield bearer). When he reached 'full age' he took part in a ceremony to become a knight. As the holder of a knight's fee his duty was to fight when called upon to do so. He was required if necessary to bring arms, armour and a horse for up to 40 days active service each year, which was expensive. Like most other medieval services, this was gradually changed to a money payment. Estates which comprised only a fraction of a knight's fee were freeholds with the same liberties from the main manor but making a proportionately smaller contribution in money or aid to the king.

As well as Budbury, Bradford manor included Cumberwell (a separate estate by 1086 and a knight's fee in 1221-2), Atworth (a quarter of a knight's fee by 1242-3), Little Atworth or Cottles (a separate estate in 1086 and a third of a knight's fee in 1242-3), Chalfield (a separate estate in 1086) and Barley to the north of South Wraxall (a fifth of a knight's fee in 1242-3).

In 1001 King Ethelred II gave the remainder of Bradford manor (that is, without Wingfield, Westwood and Monkton Farleigh) to the nuns of Shaftesbury Abbey in Dorset.

He said this was to provide a safe refuge for the nuns and for the bones of Edward the Martyr, murdered at Corfe in 978 and buried at Shaftesbury the following year.[3] The nuns might well have needed a refuge because of the regular incursions by Vikings landing on the south coast. Bradford was further inland than Shaftesbury and perhaps the king had the River Avon and the hillfort at Budbury in mind as defences.

Domesday book

Vlf teñ . I . hid in *BODEBERIE* . Tra . ē . I . car̄ . ⁊ Valet . c . folid.
Ibi ſt . IIII . bord ⁊ III . ſerui . ⁊ III . ac filuæ . Valet . x . folid.

Ulf holds 1 hide in BUDBURY. Land for 1 plough.
   4 smallholders and 3 slaves.
   Woodland, 3 acres.
Value 10s.

Fig. 8: Domesday book entry

The first description of Budbury is in the Domesday book of 1086 (fig.8). An Anglo-Saxon thane called Ulf (meaning wolf) held the freehold estate of one hide. A hide was a sufficient acreage to support a well-off household and their retainers. The size varied with the quality of the land but in this area was probably 80 to 120 acres. Domesday book says there was arable land at Budbury sufficient for one plough. There were also three acres of woodland. Ulf's tenants were four bordars and three serfs. The annual value of his holding was 10 shillings. Bordars were cottagers farming marginal land taken in from wasteland or woodland. Serfs were unfree tenants tied to the manor. They paid a small rent for their holding which included some acres in the common field, some grazing and a share of meadow. They were obliged to carry out seasonal and other farmwork for their lord.

This was Ulf's only holding in 1086 but Woolley which was written 'Wlfleg' in 1242 (Ulf's Leigh) may link him also with that part of Bradford.

Ulf's gift of Budbury to Shaftesbury

After 1066 knights' fees usually remained in a family and were inherited. Ulf gifted Budbury to Shaftesbury Abbey for the soul of his wife and from this time on, though it remained a freehold, it was held under the Abbey rather than directly under the king, paying an annual chief rent to the Abbey. The gift may not have taken effect immediately or may have been blocked by the king. It was described as a purchase when it was confirmed in 1122 that Emma, Abbess of Shaftesbury, had bought one and a half hides of land in Bradford and Budbury from Ulf's successor, Robert Sacon and his sons.[4] The inclusion of the sons in the deed was to prevent Robert's heirs disputing the sale. The purchase was confirmed by King Henry I (1100-1135) as overlord.[5] At first Sacon rented back the extra ½ hide, which was at Bradford Leigh in Holt tithing but later he gave it up.

Between 1127 and 1130, a survey made for the abbey lists Sacon no longer holding Budbury but paying 15d rent for a house in the borough of Bradford and two acres of land. He was now one of the Abbess's messengers. The 1½ hides of the estate were held by Ailric Palmer who paid 20s for the Budbury hide, 8s for the ½ hide in Leigh tithing and 2s for his house. The name 'palmer' indicates someone who wore a palm branch as a token that they had made a pilgrimage to the Holy Land.

In another survey made in about 1170, the one hide estate was in hand and temporarily held by Colstan, priest of Bradford, paying the 20s rent.[6] One of the men who helped to make the survey was Alfric Munuc or monk. He was also called Alfric of the Well, possibly living at Lady Well. He may not have been a true monk as he held a virgate of land paying 4s rent. He had some customary duties; to plough, fallow and reap an acre of manorial land, carry messages for the Abbess and do carriage duty, driving a wagon to Shaftesbury before the feasts of Christmas and Easter.

The de Budbury family

A third survey of 1190-1200 shows the Budbury estate held by William 'de Buddebere'.[7] He probably also had a family name but he was known by the name of his estate as was the custom. He was one of the three men in Winsley tithing who had to organise two Scot Ales annually to raise money for the church.[8] He also had to attend a 'tourn' or court and he held some land in Atworth tithing. At the same date a half virgate in the borough was held by Gilbert de Budebere for 4s 8d rent and 2d for a market stall and toll.[9] He was taxed ½d for 'Sheriff's Aid'.[10] In a charter of about 1200-1216 between Abbess Mary of Shaftesbury and Roger of Wraxall, Gilbert was one of the witnesses which shows his standing locally.[11]

The description or nickname Monk persisted. In 1190 there were three men living in Winsley tithing, perhaps brothers and descendants of Alfric Munuc alias Alfric of the Well. They were Athelinus monachus who held the virgate of land which had been Alfric's with the additional responsibility of providing help with the abbey's hay harvest, Willelmus (William) monachus who held half a virgate (about 14 acres) and had to carry out labouring work four days a week and every day at harvest, in return for an allowance of grain on Thursdays and Radus (Ralph) monachus who had even less land and more labouring duties.

The open fields

Like most early land holdings, the manor's arable and other land was not in a single block but dispersed amongst other holdings. North of Winsley Road lay the common arable field called Berryfield or Bearfield, bere meant corn as in the words 'barn' and 'barton'. It may have been the original 'ploughland' of Budbury. It extended to Bath Road on the east side and as far north-west as Little Ashley. Open fields were divided into groups of strips called 'furlongs'. Cock Stile at the north end and Cumberland west of Frankleigh were two of the Bearfield furlongs.

There was another open plough field west of Wine Street called Hare Knapp. This steep area was perhaps developed from former common grazing shared by the inhabitants of Bradford, Budbury and Winsley. It was divided by Belcombe Brook. Budbury manor had strips of land in both Bearfield and Hare Knapp.

Transfers of land and references to woodland

From the early 13th century there appear to have been two families with holdings at Budbury. In 1208 Robert, son of Maisy, granted William de Budbury a quarter of a wood in 'Budebury towards the south', perhaps meaning the south part of the wood.[12] ('Maisy' as a name is derived from a Norman place-name, either Maizy in Aisne or Maisy in Calvados.) The same year Robert Gerveys of Buddebury, (the same Robert, son of Maisy? Gervys was the Germanic personal name Gervase, brought by the Normans and common in the 12th and 13th centuries, later the family name Jarvis) conveyed to William Hall of Bradford and his wife Katherine, for 20s, a piece of land in Berefeld called Garston between the land of John de Ashley and John de Bradford and nigh Buddebury Wood. The Halls, who lived on the east side of the town above the town mill, held the main sub-manor of Bradford. The witnesses to the deed were surrounding landholders: Sir John de Holte, Sir John de Comerwelle, Walter de Chaldfield, John Basset and others. This is the first time Bearfield is mentioned and shows that some strips belonged to properties in Bradford borough and Ashley. Garston is a common place-name meaning a paddock or grass enclosure so this part of Bearfield had already been enclosed. Budbury wood was located immediately west of the Roman villa site. In later references its name was Great Woods.

The hermit

In the 13th century there is the first reference to a hermit associated with Ladywell spring, a holy well in Newtown at the foot of Budbury hill.[13] This was a key natural feature of the town. Holy wells were especially prevalent in Celtic areas, particularly Brittany and Wales and were associated with healing. There was a tradition at Bradford that the water at Ladywell was good for eye complaints.

Representatives of Bradford Hundred at the Wiltshire Eyre, (a criminal court held by royal justices), reported in 1268 that Richard le Wood and Richard le Eremite had quarrelled. Richard le Wode had knifed the hermit in the stomach and he had later died. Richard le Wode fled to Wingfield. He had no possessions which could be seized as a fine and he was outlawed. The next reference to a hermit is in 1428 when the Abbess of Shaftesbury gave 4d to 'a hermit' at Bradford.

Hermits pursued a religious life in isolation rather than within a monastic community. However, they sometimes served as guides to wayfarers or as ferrymen. Either of these roles would have been possible at Bradford where pilgrims passed through on the way to Glastonbury and the river Avon had to be crossed. They sometimes lived in natural caves or a dwelling carved out of a cliff and again there is a shelter carved out of the quarry face above Ladywell which has traditionally been associated with the hermit (fig.9).

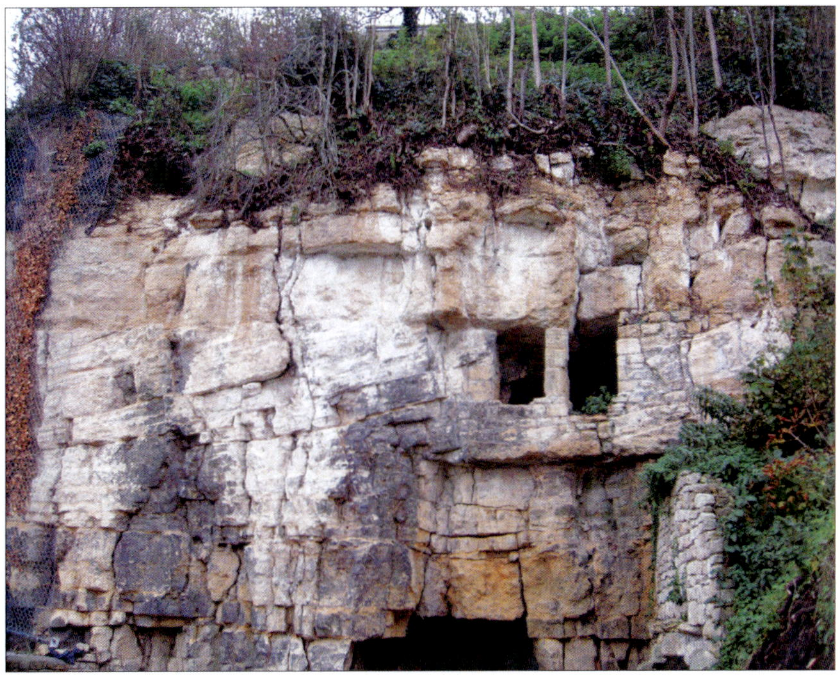

Fig. 9: The hermit's cave, 2014

Another feature associated with hermits is a chapel and we have the cruciform St. Mary Tory chapel and hospice directly above the rock dwelling. By tradition, the hermit descended from the chapel via a passage in the rock to this cave where he received pilgrims but though the back of the cave has a blocked passage, the top end of a passage has not been found. A 19th century drawing of the east end of the chapel and an early photograph show a doorway in the north-east corner which could have led down to the cave (fig.10).

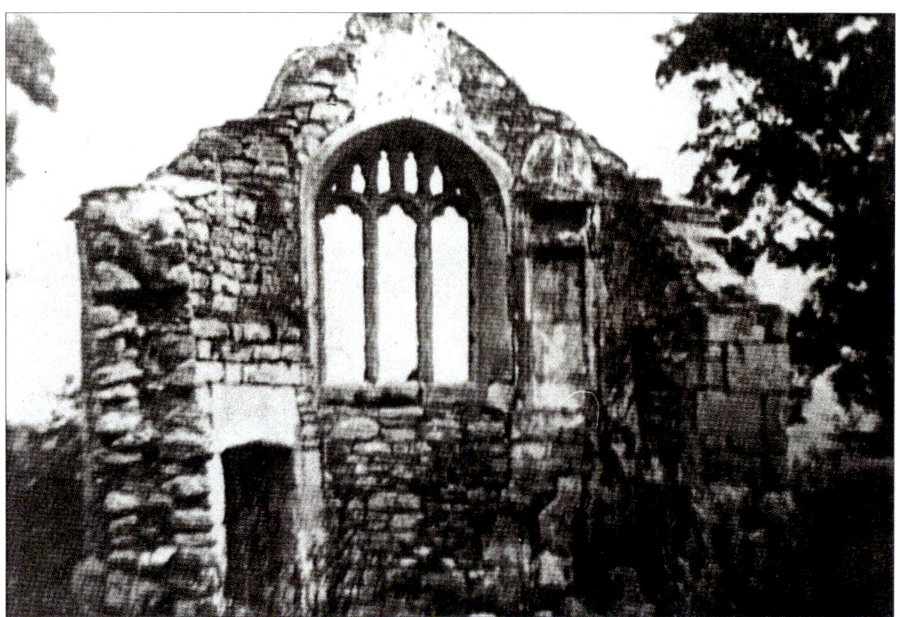

Fig. 10: Chapel interior c. 1860 with corner doorway and niche

The pilgrim route from the north passed through two other hospices. Firstly, Chapel Plaister at Box which has 15th century buildings and then St Audoen's Chapel at South Wraxall where the hospice building of about 1300 survives as a farmhouse but the chapel has gone. The chapel at St Mary Tory was formerly dedicated to St Leonard, especially associated with small chapels in woods and remote places. The windows and highly decorated niche date it to the 15th century. We do not know if there was an earlier chapel on the site. Late 14th century accounts of Shaftesbury Abbey state that the 'house of St. Mary' was excused its rent of 12d but this has not been identified.[14] When the antiquarian Leland visited the town in 1533 he reported, 'There is a chapel on the highest place of the town as I entered.' In the 17th century John Aubrey, who also visited Bradford, described St Mary Tory as 'The finest hermitage in England.' This was quite an accolade from a man who visited antiquities all over the country.

Further references to the two Budbury families

In 1278 at another court called trailbaston and gaol delivery, at Old Salisbury gaol twelve men from Bradford hundred were fined for non-appearance.[15] They included Walter de Budbury who was fined ½ mark (40d) and Gervase de Budbury fined 5s.

The half hide at Bradford Leigh became detached from the Budbury estate. In 1304 a deed called a 'fine' or final concord confirmed that John de Buddebury had sold to John de Bradeford and his wife Isabel for 100 marks, a house and 2 virgates (½ hide) of land in Bradford.[16] This came with the homage and all the services of several tenants: Robert

Gervys, Nicholas the dyer of Bradford and his wife Margery, and Stephen de la Slade. The latter may have held what became Slade's Farm at Bradford Leigh. As part of the same transaction John de Buddebury granted to John de Bradeford the 'remainder' (i.e. the right to take on after the present holder) of 2 acres, which James the carpenter and his wife Christine held for their lives and 2 acres which Nicholas the dyer and his wife Margery held for their lives. These had been inherited by John de Buddebury from an earlier man of the same name.[17] It was recorded that Robert Gerveys had done homage and fealty to his new lord, John de Bradeford, as had the tenants Nicholas, Margery, James, Christine and Stephen. Robert Gervys is likely to have been the same man or a descendant of Gervase de Budbury.

Tax list of 1332

There were 24 taxpayers in Bradford borough tithing but as many as 35 in Winsley (which included Limpley Stoke as well as Budbury).[18] Amongst the Winsley tithing, neither the name Budbury nor the name Gervys occurs but there were William atte Putte (well), John le Palmere and Reynold le Moneke, all names which have been mentioned above.

3 Budbury manor is joined with Ashley manor

Ashley manor

In the early 15th century the Budbury estate was combined with the Great Ashley estate, to the north of Winsley. Ashley was not a separate manor at the time of Domesday Book unlike Budbury and Cumberwell. It appears first in the Shaftesbury survey of Bradford manor made in about 1170. At that time Reginald de Aslega held just half a virgate, a very small farm.[1] He paid a rent of 15d a year and had an obligation to reap half an acre of manorial land.[2] In the 1190 survey the holder was Walter de Haslega, in 1208 it was John of Ashley and in 1280 Roger de Asselegh. The Ashley family gained more land and in 1327 and again in 1332, John de Asshleye was the second highest taxpayer in Winsley tithing showing a considerable increase in prosperity.[3] In 1356 Reginald Ashley, perhaps a younger son, and his wife Joan conveyed two houses and land in Upper and Lower Westwood to William of Iford.[4] The same year John de Ashley who held the Ashley estate witnessed deeds in Bradford[5] and in November 1360 witnessed an Edington Priory deed. [6] At the time of the poll tax in 1377 he was a freeholder paying 6s 8d for the estate, the wealthiest man at Winsley.[7] Ashley, being a large freehold property, was now accounted a sub-manor.

We know that John Ashley married Edith, daughter and heir of John Talbot of Salisbury.[8] Her father originally lived at Trowbridge and in 1328 acquired land belonging to John de la Grove.[9] Three fields have his name at Studley Green. (Talbot and Grove remain today as street names.) In 1365 John Talbot settled his property in Trowbridge and Salisbury on his grandsons, the sons of John and Edith. In exchange the couple provided him with an annuity of £59 and competent food and lodging for him and for his servants whenever he should come to the Grove.[10] In 1374, probably after his death, a jury enquired as to whether he had held lands at 'la Grove' and it was reported at the next court that he had granted them to his relative John Ashley.

John and Edith seem to have moved to Salisbury. The Trowbridge property was sufficient to be considered a sub-manor of the manor of Trowbridge and was called Trowbridge Ashleys. It included two properties in Hill Street. The Ashley-Cooper family retained it until the reign of Elizabeth I and later it was absorbed into the manor of Trowbridge Dauntsey which eventually was joined to the Hall estate of Bradford.

Robert Ashley

The eldest son of John and Edith Ashley was Robert and as well as Ashley he inherited the properties at Trowbridge and Salisbury from his mother's family.[11] His career suggests he had legal training as a young man and he rose to prominence in Wiltshire and further afield. He is first recorded in 1403 and 1405 when he witnessed the sale of a house in Pippet Street, Bradford.[12] He witnessed other deeds in 1414 and 1430.[13] From 1414 he was joint lessee of the duchy of Lancaster lordship of Trowbridge and a fishery on the River Avon at Staverton. From 1414 to 1432 he was Verderer of Pewsham and Melksham Forests and from 1424 to 1432 of Blackmore Forest. In 1418 he was fined 12 marks for marrying, without the necessary licence. This was to Gillian Plecy, the widow of John Plecy of Shapwick Plecy in Dorset, a tenant-in-chief of the crown who had died in 1416. She held the manor of Wimborne St. Giles in Dorset in her own right as the only daughter and heir of Sir John Hamelyn who died in 1398. The Latin form of her name is Egidia, the female version of Giles, the patron saint of her father's manor. Wimbourne was later the seat of the well-known Ashley-Cooper family, created Earls of Shaftesbury in 1672.

Robert Ashley's career continued. He became an MP for Wiltshire in 1419. In 1426-1427 he was escheator for Hampshire and Wiltshire. In this important office he oversaw property that fell to a lord of the manor or the state, for lack of an heir or because of forfeiture.[14] In this role he was succeeded by another local man, Robert Long of South Wraxall Manor.

The exact date and circumstances of Budbury manor joining with Ashley manor are unknown. In 1414 we have the last reference to the Budbury family. Reynold Buddebury was one of the local witnesses to a deed granting the manor of Tellisford, Somerset, to trustees. Interestingly Robert Asshelegh was one of the other witnesses.[15] It is likely that he acquired Budbury at about this time as when he became an MP he was described as 'of Budbury'.

Budbury manor house, now 4 Budbury Place, has origins in this period and Robert as the holder of considerable property and public offices is likely to have built a fine new house. Stone was becoming more available for house building gradually replacing timber-framing in the area. The former manor house was of stone and had a three-room and cross passage plan. It retains fragments of a 15th century open arch-braced collar truss which would have been over the open hall, stretches of thick walling and the moulded jamb of a medieval entrance doorway (fig.11).

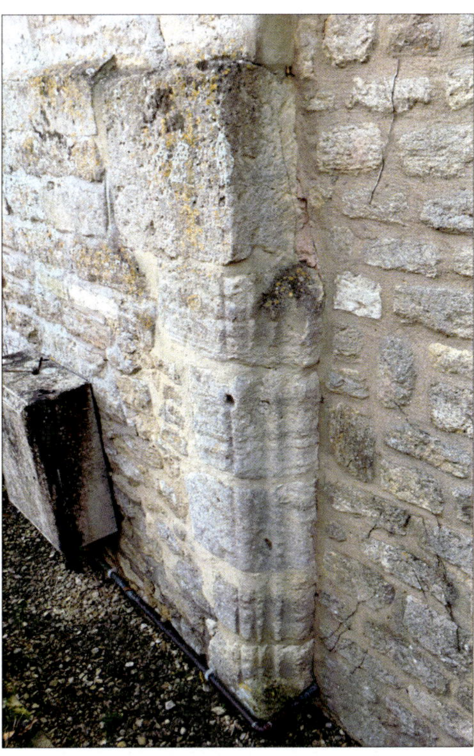

Fig. 11: Jamb of a medieval doorway at Budbury Manor (WBR)

Robert died shortly before 20th April 1433. His widow Gillian married a third time, to Sir Thomas Thame of Hampshire. She died in 1476. Robert and Gillian had two sons, Edmund recorded in about 1460-80 and Robert of Cranborne, Dorset who married Isabel but died childless before 1476. Hugh, perhaps Edmund's son, was born in about 1465 and died 29th April 1493.[16] His estates passed to his eldest son who became Sir Henry Ashley. In 1493 Budbury and Ashley were shown combined in the court book of Bradford manor.[17]

4   The Sixteenth Century

On the dissolution of Shaftesbury Abbey in 1539 the manor of Bradford, including the sub-manor of Ashley and Budbury, fell to the crown. It was leased first to Sir Edward Bellingham, Lord Deputy of Ireland, and subsequently to the Earl of Pembroke and Sir Francis Walsingham. Barton Farm was held separately from 1574 on a 21 year lease by Stephen Blanchard alias Sanshue or Sanghewe. Throughout this time the Ashleys, although no longer living locally, continued to own the freehold of the sub-manor of Ashley and Budbury. Their holding of Ashley was confirmed by a Letter Patent when Walsingham acquired the manor of Bradford.

Westbury family

<table>
<tr><td colspan="3" align="center">Richard Westbury m. Joan m. – Reynolds</td></tr>
<tr><td align="center">d.1557</td><td align="center">d.1572</td><td align="center">d. before 1572</td></tr>
<tr><td colspan="3" align="center">|</td></tr>
<tr><td colspan="3" align="center">William Reynolds alias Westbury m. (2) Elizabeth</td></tr>
<tr><td colspan="3" align="center">(yeoman of Budbury) d. 1586</td></tr>
<tr><td colspan="3" align="center">|</td></tr>
<tr><td colspan="3" align="center">William
d. 1598
(husbandman)</td></tr>
</table>

Fig. 12

In 1546 their tenant of Budbury manor was Richard Westbury, one of only three taxpayers in Winsley.[1] His will, in which he was called 'of Budbury', was proved in 1557.[2] He left 4d to Salisbury Cathedral and 6s 8d to the parish church of Bradford. He had two young sons, Walter and Henry who were left 40 marks each 'to be delivered at such time as it shall be thought most needful' by the executors. He left 20 marks each to his young daughters Alice the elder and Alice the younger, to be paid to them on the day of their marriage 'so that [if] they marry by the advice and consent of my executors'. Richard also had an older son called after his father and two sheep were left to 'Richard Westbury my son's son' and to Agnes his daughter. Bartolomew Pickering, son of James Pickering, and Bartolomew Paynter, son of Richard's sister were also left one sheep each. His friends Henry Deverell and John Dance who were to supervise the will were each left 13s 4d. The rest was left to his wife Joan.

On 12th November 1570 Joan Westbury alias Reynolds, widow, wrote her will.[3] She was now the tenant of the Budbury estate. She probably held it for her widowhood after Richard Westbury's death and she may have remarried, to a man called Reynolds who had also died. Her first bequest was to her sister Elizabeth: ten shillings, a furnished bed, a crock, a pan and all her linen and woollen clothes. The next bequests were to her children: to William 20 shillings and all her 'yoting' stones, to Walter 20 sheep, 20 bushels of barley, a crock and a pan, to Alice Lewyn 20s and to Alice Pykeringe 20s. The two daughters named Alice show that Joan was indeed the widow of Richard Westbury. She also made bequests of 2 bushels of wheat and 2 of malt to Richard Westbury (probably the grandson mentioned in her husband's will), the same to Joan Westbury and to Cicely Westbury (probably Richard's sisters, her grand-daughters). One bushel of wheat and one of malt were left to Agnes Storage (perhaps the daughter Agnes mentioned by Richard, now married). Each of the children of her other daughter Alice Pyckering was left a sheep. Other bequests were: a bushel of wheat and one of malt, a coverlet and a blanket to Goodwife Jeyles, 2s to Thomas Lynte, 12d to Mays and the same to John D-nycke the younger, a yearling heifer to her servant Jane and finally 6d each to the poor people of St. Margaret's almshouse, (the former leper hospital, at the end of Frome Road). The residue of her estate was left to her son Henry, who was her executor and the will was overseen by James and Anthony Pickering, probably her son-in-law and his son. They also witnessed the will along with her son Walter and others.[4]

Joan's will shows that growing arable crops and malting were the main farming activity at the manor house at this date. The bequests include twenty bushels of barley, eight bushels of wheat, eight bushels of malt and a yoting stone or steeping trough for wetting barley before malting. More than 20 sheep were left but only one heifer. We do not know what the residue of the estate comprised in addition but dairying does not seem to have been important.

Sale by the Ashleys of the combined Ashley and Budbury estates to John Blanchard in 1579

In 1578 the sub-manor of Ashley and Budbury was sold by the Ashleys to John Blanchard, a wealthy yeoman or gentleman of Marshfield, Gloucestershire.[5] He could have been related to the Stephen Blanchard of Barton Farm but, to date, no connection has been found and hardly anything is known about Stephen.

By the deed, dated 15th Aug. 1578, Sir Henry Ashley of Upper Wimborne St Giles, Dame Katherine his wife, Henry Ashley his son and heir and Anthony Ashley of Damerham, Wilts gent., brother of Sir Henry, conveyed to John Blanchard for £620 all those the capital messuages, tenements or farms commonly called by the name of the Manor of Ashley and Budbury, Wiltshire with all houses, lands, buildings, orchards, gardens, tofts, dovehouses, lands, tenements, meadows, leasows, pastures, commons, woods etc. reversions etc. and the perquisites of Court whatsoever they be, in the Parish of Bradford now being in the tenure, maintenance or occupation of John Carter and Anthony Carter or their assigns [at Ashley] or in the tenure of William Reynolds alias Westbury or his assigns [at Budbury]. So nine years after the death of Joan, William Reynolds alias Westbury, her son held the estate. (When manors were tenanted they were called 'farm', so the house at Budbury was described as the 'capital messuage' – the principal house – of Budbury Farm.)

Anthony Carter alias Druce, tenant of Ashley married Margaret Blanchard, John's sister.[6] The couple lived at Little Ashley. Great Ashley was the home of Anthony's brother John, who, in another neat arrangement, married Edith, another of John Blanchard's sisters.

Death of William Reynolds alia Westbury

A son of William Reynolds alias Westbury may be the William 'son of William' who was buried at Holy Trinity on August 13th 1586. William Westbury 'senior', described as yeoman of Bradford, wrote his will on 27th September 1586.[7] His wife was Elizabeth and his children Robert, William, Eleanor and Alice, all 'by his last wife', were under age. This suggests Elizabeth was his second wife and that by her he had a second son called William. The overseers of the will were Anthony Druce (of Ashley) and Anthony Pickering, probably the grandson of Joan Westbury alias Reynolds. William was buried at Holy Trinity on 4th October that year.

William Westbury alias Reynolds, the second son of that name, was buried at Holy Trinity, Bradford on 19th May 1598 and an inventory of his goods was taken the same day by John Druce, Roger Deverill, John Baylie, John Dicke senior, John Dicke junior and John Westbury. It is very beautifully written by someone used to writing legal documents. In it he is described as a husbandman of Bradford. The manor house was in a rundown state. The names of the ten rooms indicate an originally good quality house with a two-storey porch but although there was a kitchen it was not used for cooking, only to store a few items. The house now operated as a farmhouse rather than the manor house it had been.

Other houses of the Budbury estate

The sale to Blanchard by the Ashleys included in the Budbury estate one other messuage or tenement in the tenure or occupation of Thomas Phillips and another tenement with an orchard, garden and a close of pasture adjoining estimated to be 2 ½ acres in Bradford and 12 acres of land in the fields of Bradford, now in the tenure of James Newman at a rent of 8[s?], this last was perhaps Gregories in Whiteheads Lane. There was also a cottage with a garden plot and backside lying under Catsholehill, now in the tenure or occupation of Thomas Litecombe for life. This hill is the quarry cliff at Newtown below the Hermitage and the cottage may have been a quarryman's.

The Hermitage

Apart from the manor house and its lands, Sir Henry Ashley also sold John Blanchard 'all that messuage or tenement called the Hermytage' with an orchard, garden and little copse to the same belonging and lying in Bradford, now in the tenure or occupation of William Reynolds alias Westbury held by the yearly rent of 13s. When Leland, Henry VIII's antiquary, visited Bradford in 1533, checking up on ecclesiastical property, he said; 'There is a chapel on the highest place of the town as I entered'. We do not know what happened to the resident hermit at the Dissolution but the Hermitage passed into secular use and became attached to Budbury manor. In 1587 a quitclaim was signed by John Barker, a Bristol merchant, renouncing any claim on the hermitage, described as St. Leonard's hermitage or chapel lying near Catsholshill.[8] This implies that it had initially been granted to him after the Dissolution and that he had sold it to the Ashleys. The deed is endorsed with a note that livery of seisin had been carried out in the presence of John Druce of Ashley. This was a process demonstrating the transfer of property by the meeting of the two parties or their representatives at the site and a handful of soil being given to the new owner.

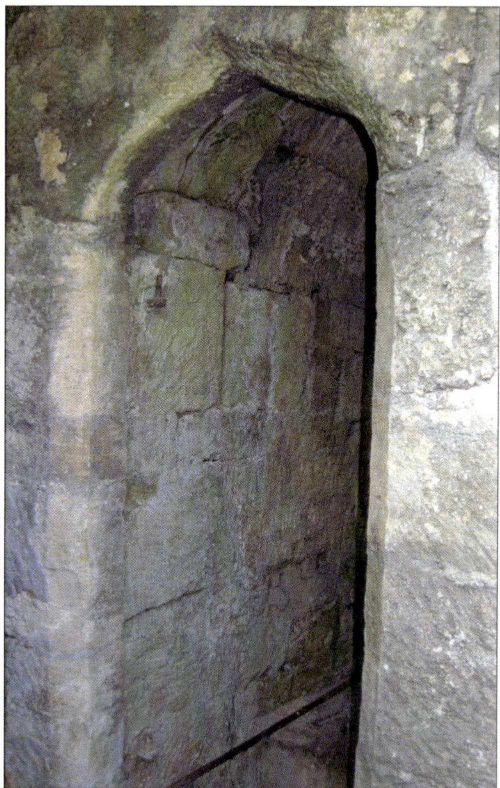

Ladywell

The spring at the foot of Budbury hill is the most important one in the town (a second one, Pippetts Well, is in Market Street). It is likely to have been a pagan sacred site and it is significant that the Iron Age and Roman sites and the medieval hermitage site at St. Mary Tory are immediately above it and the Saxon Church and Holy Trinity are in line between it and the river. The spring site was protected by a wellhouse with an arched doorway (fig. 13). There was also an open dipping well, a shallow stone trough, south of Ladywell Cottage on the other side of the road. The stream running between the spring and the open well is visible through an inspection glass in Ladywell Cottage.

Fig. 13: Doorway into the wellhouse at Lady Well

5   The Seventeenth Century

John Blanchard junior

After the death of William Reynolds alias Westbury in 1586 it seems likely that the manor house remained with his wife Elizabeth during her widowhood. If the inventory of her son taken in 1598 was at the time of her death this may have brought the family's lease to an end causing the manor to revert to the Blanchards. John Blanchard, son of John Blanchard of Marshfield, now came to live at Budbury, close to his relatives at Ashley. As 'John Blanchard of Budbury', he was listed amongst the Wiltshire freeholders in 1607-8. After his father's death he also inherited the two Ashley properties.

We have seen that the Budbury manor house was in a rundown state and this is probably the time when it was rebuilt in the more compact form we see today. It has good stone fireplaces, ovolo-moulded mullioned windows, two storeys and a habitable attic, lit by a gable dormer window (figs. 14-16). The large width of the house, front to back, is another sign of its quality. It may have been John Blanchard who, as a gentleman, set up a park in the land immediately surrounding the house and he may also have built or altered the Barton or farmyard complex, north-east of the house. The name Budbury Farm associated with that site is additional evidence that it was the home farm of Budbury Manor. It comprised at this period a wagon house, stable and stalls. The wall thicknesses of the two surviving ranges make a late 16th century or early 17th century date likely but the walls are battered (wider at the foot) which is a typical 15th century feature. A stone pillar, now indoors, but formerly outside the west range, is an interesting high quality feature (fig.17). In 1925 some masonry was still attached to the back of it and it appears to be in situ. It is moulded at the foot but not well defined enough now to help with dating. Its most likely function was as a flat buttress at the corner of the west range. The original uses of the ranges have been lost through alterations. The west range roof probably dates from the 17th century and the main range the early 18th century.

Burgages and cottages belonging to Budbury

In around 1600, John Blanchard paid a rent of 3s 1½d to Bradford manor for two burgages at the south end of 'Pepit' Street 'sometime in the occupation of Robert Boucher and now in the tenure of Robert Fipp [Phipp]'.[1] This may be the Robert 'Fyppe' tailor who accidentally shot George Cutbert , a mercer, when they were shooting together at the archery butts on 14th June 1573.[2] George died a week later. Robert was pardoned by the Justices at a hearing the following February. He may have been a son-in-law or grandson of Joan Reynolds alias Westbury whose daughter Edith married a Phipp.

John Blanchard 'of Budbury gent' granted leases of two properties in Newtown in October 1607.[3] The first concerned a tenement at Catteshill leased to Edward Mitchell,

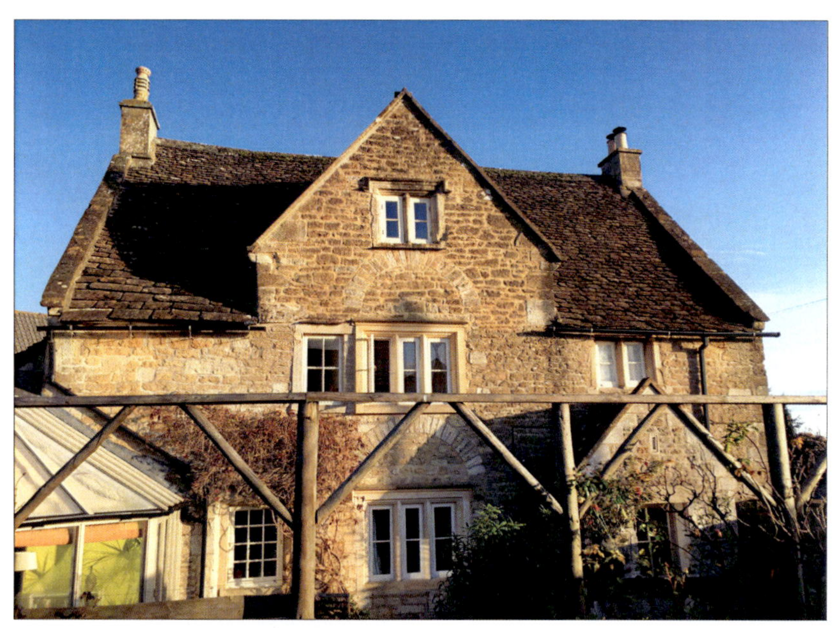

Above, Fig. 14: Budbury Manor (Peter Mann)

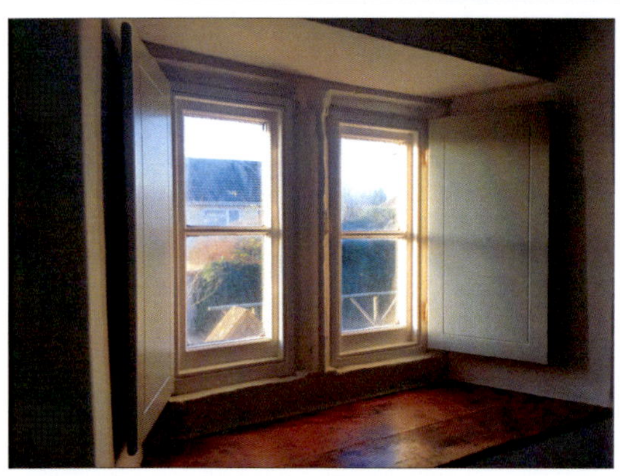

Left, Fig. 15: Mullioned window (Peter Mann)

Below left, Fig. 16: First floor fireplace (Jane Mann)

Below right, Fig. 17: The pillar at Budbury Farm (WBR)

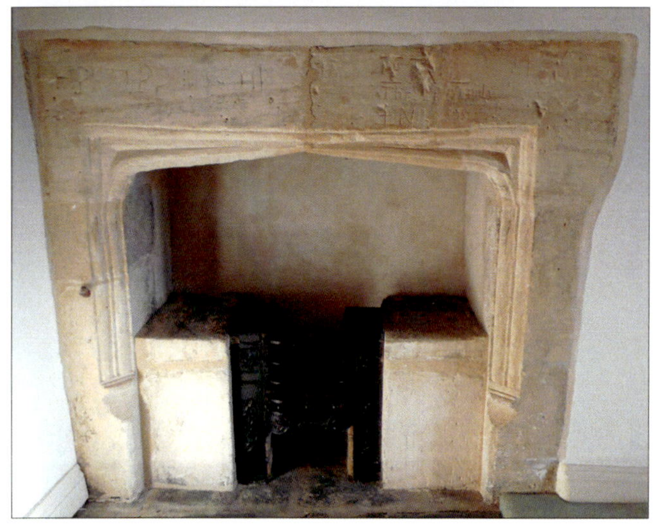

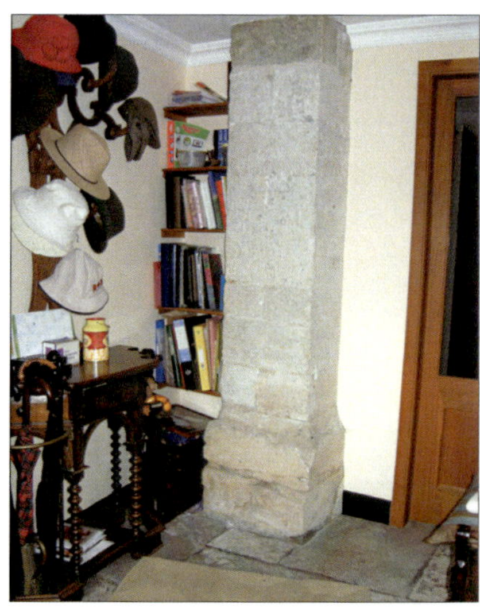

carpenter. Mitchell had built it himself and occupied it. He also leased an area of garden. Whether he had built the house with permission is not stated. The second lease was to Paul Mason of Bradford, freemason, of a house with an orchard and garden at Catteshill.[4] This may be the cottage previously occupied by Thomas Litecombe and confirms that it housed a quarryman. Building firms required both masons and carpenters, so Edward Mitchell may have been working with Paul Mason.

On 1st December the same year John Blanchard leased to Richard Marchant of Catteshill, labourer, a cottage at Catteshill 'in consideration of the new erecting and late building of the cottage' by Marchant.[5] Marchant had petitioned the Justices of the Peace at Salisbury that he was 'destitute of habitation' and had obtained a licence from them to erect the cottage 'where he dwelleth' with a little garden and backside.[6] His petition with named supporters is dated 7th January 1607. Under an Elizabethan statute it was illegal to build cottages without at least four acres of land to provide some means of subsistence. It is reasonable to suppose that Marchant was labouring in the quarry.

The death of John Blanchard

John did not have many years to enjoy the rebuilt house, perhaps constructed with stone from his own quarry in Newtown. He made his will on 18th March 1611, being 'sick in body' and it was proved on 5th September.[7] He was again described as 'gentleman of Budbury'. He may have fallen victim to one of the episodes of plague. Certainly in 1609 Bradford was severely affected. The town appealed after 20 weeks to Quarter Sessions for additional aid. Places within 5 miles of the town had already been taxed and now Chippenham, Melksham and Whorwelsdown hundred were also ordered to help.

John was buried in Bradford church on March 21st, leaving the church 5s 8d. He left his three daughters, Elizabeth Blanchard, Susan Blanchard and Joyce Blanchard £20 each when they reached the age of 14. After the death of his wife Elizabeth, he willed that his son John Blanchard should have all the bedsteads 'in my house with all the table boards, benches, forms, tacks, livery boards, cupboards, stools, maltstones, one chest, two wains with their 'furniture', two cutts [carts?], two dungpots, all my rick staddles with all my plough harness whatever and all the decks and planks and all such implements that doth belong to my stables and stalls. My said son shall have my best bed and bedstead with his [its] furniture thereunto belonging in the broad chamber.' He gave the poor folks of Bradford 5s 8d and the poor folks of Marshfield the same. His wife Elizabeth was to be executrix and the overseers of the will were William Richmond and Edward Wenyard alias England. The witnesses were Robert Horlock, Edward Richman and John Prittle. Richman or Richmond was the maiden name of his wife so William and Edward were her relatives.

In 1619 Walter Long of Whaddon near Hilperton, a younger brother of the lord of the manor of Whaddon, renewed the lease of a cottage at Upper Paxcroft in Steeple

Ashton parish to John Blanchard, Elizabeth his wife and their son John.[8] The lease would have been made before John's death in 1611. As his son John died in 1613 the only ' life' now remaining on the lease was Elizabeth's. The property was by the Paxcroft Brook, used for processes in cloth making. The Paxcroft estate had been leased to a William Blanchard who died in 1566[9] and his son William then inherited but was bought out by Walter Long in about 1616. It seems very likely that John Blanchard of Budbury was related to these Blanchards.

Elizabeth Blanchard: quarrying and a rabbit warren

John's widow Elizabeth continued to live at Budbury and did not remarry. On 28th March 1628 she leased a cottage at Catsholehill alias Catshill to Thomas Bishop of Southampton, yeoman.[10] It was described as having two fields of housing (that is two bays), adjoining to the north end of a cottage there occupied by John Florence. The lease also included a plot of ground extending from the chimney of this cottage round to the north end of the same cottage and up to the Coniger there. She reserved for her own use the stones and the 'quarr, of and for the digging of stones, on the little plot of ground' along with the right of free 'egress and regress' from time to time to dig, take and carry away stones without annoyance to the cottage. Bishop also leased another little plot or garden there between the cottage held by Maud Burgess widow on the north and a cottage on the south now or before held by John Nicholls. This deed is the first direct evidence of quarrying and the associated building of a group of cottages at the foot of Budbury hill.

It is also the first reference to the coniger or rabbit warren on the hill south east of the manor house, using land unsuitable for agriculture. Warrens are often medieval in origin and required a grant of 'free warren' from the king to a lord of the manor. The Abbess of Shaftesbury, the overlord of Budbury, received such a grant in 1293 but we do not know the exact date when this warren was established or the larger one in the Borough tithing on the east side of Conigre Hill (later becoming Priory Park). Rabbits were valuable for their meat and their fur. They were confined within a walled or fenced area with their burrows in low rectangular pillow mounds, usually at right angles to the slope of the hill to help drainage.[11]

The three Blanchard sisters

Elizabeth's son and heir John had died in July 1613 so his three sisters became wards of court. Wardships were sold by the Crown and the person acquiring the 'wardship and marriage' often arranged for the ward to marry a relative. Wardship of the sisters was granted to Mr James Capp.[12] When their mother died in January 1630 the Ashley and Budbury estate was divided, as was the custom, amongst the three, Susannah, Elizabeth and Joyce, all of whom were now married (fig.18). Their husbands would hold their share of the property 'in right of their wives'. The freehold estate comprised one messuage

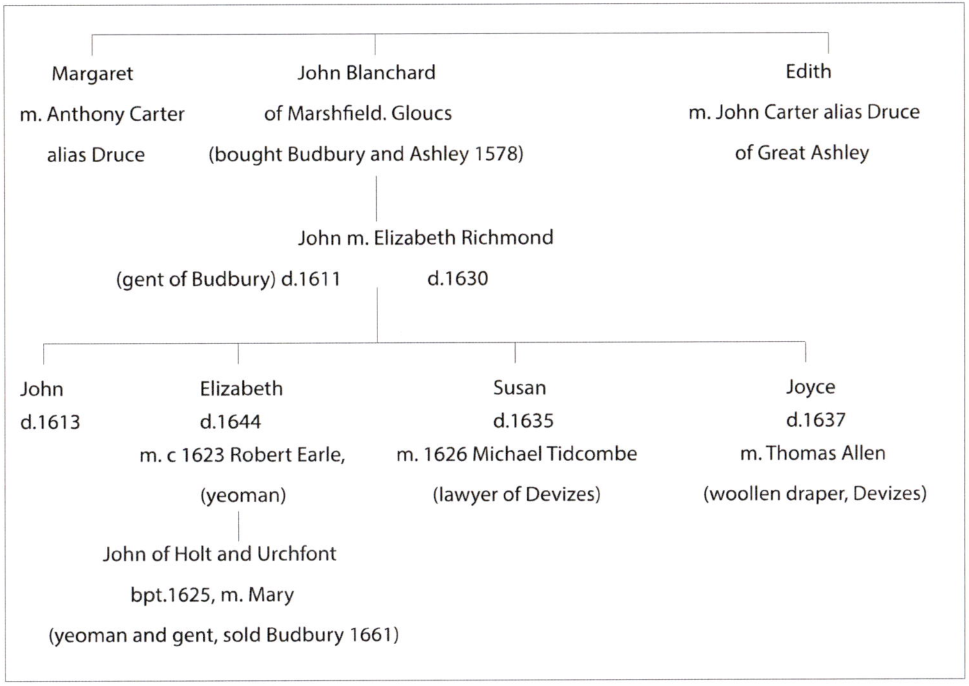

Fig. 18: Blanchard family

and four yardlands called Great Ashley, held by the service of a fourth part of a knight's fee and 10s annual rent and 2s in lieu of 'earing' , ploughing four acres of the lord's land yearly, and by suit of court to the Bradford Hundred court from 3 weeks to 3 weeks and yielding a 'mortuary' after the death of the tenant of one horse with its saddle and bridle. Also one messuage and four yardlands called Budbury by service of the fourth part of a knight's fee, 20s rent and 5s Larder Money (probably in lieu of a food rent) and similar suit of court and mortuary. This description puts the Ashley and Budbury estates at very similar values except the Budbury rental value is higher.

Susannah Tidcombe

In 1626 Susannah (Susan) had married, in Bradford church, Michael Tidcombe, a gentleman and successful Devizes lawyer, son of another Michael Tidcombe who died in 1639. They lived in Devizes. Susannah was allocated the manor house at Great Ashley with a dovecote and large pond adjoining, a group of fields close to Great Ashley, a close of pasture called Budbery Great Wood of 9½ acres, a close of pasture or arable called Upper Hare Knapper of 6 acres, three parcels of land in Hare Knapper Field containing 1½ acres, five parcels of arable land in Bearfield and eight cottages in Newtown. The 'occupants'of the cottages were John Harvey, John Lacy, Mary Lewes, William White, Robert Bollen, Thomas Bishop, John Turner and Thomas Moxham. The inclusion of Thomas Bishop suggests that some of these were leaseholders who did not live there.

Susannah died in 1635 and this useful description of her personal property comes from an Inquisition *post mortem* made in 1639. A further Inquisition in 1640 determined that the eight cottages were 'held of the manor of Bradford by knight's service' showing they belonged to the submanor of Budbury.

Elizabeth Earle

Elizabeth married Robert Earle, a yeoman, in about 1623. He was one of the sons of John Earle of Holt, a freeholder in 1607-8.[13] John was the leaseholder of Holt Manor on the lives of himself and his sons John and Robert. Elizabeth was allocated Budbury 'Farm' and we know the couple lived there as her husband was described as 'of Budbury' in 1632. Their first child Sara was baptised in January 1624, followed by John in 1625, Robert in 1627, Richard in 1628, Katherine in 1634, Lucy in 1636, Edward in 1627, Thomas in 1639, Joan in 1641 and finally Joyce in 1643. Elizabeth died in 1644 and two of her daughters, Lucy and Joyce the same year. They were aged eight and one. Thomas had died in 1640 also aged about one.

Joyce Allen

Joyce, the third sister, married Thomas Allen, a Devizes woollen draper. She died on 24th March 1637 and there was an Inquisition to determine her property. She had been allocated a messuage or cottage called Gregories House with barns, buildings, garden and orchard. She also had various lands including a close of 8 acres 4 roods in Lower Hare Knapp, 2½ acres lying in Belcombe and eight cottages in Newtown. The tenants of the cottages were Anthony Burgess, Isaac Watts, Edward Mitchell, John Moore, John Florence, Cecilia Richmond, Philip Grant and John Deverell. Joyce's properties were in Winsley, Leigh, Woolley, Holt, Ashley and Bradford, all belonging to the Ashley and Budbury submanors. At that time her son John was only four years old and her husband was living at Ashley, perhaps Little Ashley. Gregories was probably in Whiteheads Lane (see below).

Other property

In 1632, the three husbands, Robert Earle, Michael Tidcombe and Thomas Allen granted two leases of cottages. This was either before the partition of the estates had been carried out or Tidcombe and Allen were included with Robert Earle to guarantee that they would not dispute the lease. The first lease on 2nd April was to John Hanney the elder, tiler for a cottage and garden in the Grove (on the side of the Budbury hill).[14] The second was to Christopher Morris of Bradford for a cottage and garden at Catshill.[15] The cottage in the Grove might possibly be 47-48 Newtown. This house appears to have older origins than the rest of the houses along Newtown and owners of no. 47 have said that their deeds go back to 1610.

Robert Earle inherited half a farm at Bradford Leigh, farmed by Thomas Kelson, from his father John, a yeoman of Holt who died in 1645.[16]

In 1647 Robert Earle and his son John who was described as 'yeoman of Holt', without the two brothers-in-law, leased to Philip Grant of Bradford, broadweaver, a cottage and garden in Catshill 'near a place called Ladywell' , late in the tenure of Robert Earle adjoining a tenement of Philip Grant on the northeast and another of his on the southwest.[17] This was the central cottage in a group of three and tells us that Robert Earle had been using it himself previously, perhaps for a farmworker. This, though surprisingly late, may be the first documentary reference to the name Ladywell. There is a further lease by John, son and heir of Robert, to Philip Grant.[18]

Rents paid to Bradford manor

In about 1655 the heirs of John Blanchard paid rents of £1 for Budbury Farm, 10s for Ashley Farm, 3s 3d for the two burgages at the south end of Pippett Street (Market Street), 5s larding money and 2s in lieu of ploughing part of the lord's demesnes.[19] At the same time John Earle junior paid 6s for freehold lands at Holt, Earles also paid for lands at Leigh and Woolley and Mr Tidcombe paid 6s 8d for lands at Winsley. Michael Tidcombe was a Royalist and lost his lands under the Parliamentarians but had regained them by this date. He died in 1662. His will included four farms; Little Ashley, one with a roofless house and two others.[20] The fields included Budbury Lye, a garden plot in Bearfield and parts of Hare Knapp.

Purchase of Budbury Farm by Paul Methuen

Paul Methuen was described by John Aubrey as the 'greatest clothier of his time'.[21] He was born at Frome in 1613. He leased the house at the top of Market Street, later called The Priory, in 1646 and began trading as a clothier from there. He bought the freehold in 1657 and John Aubrey described it as his 'seat'.[22] In 1641 he was married to Sarah but after her death he married Grace Ashe, daughter of another clothier. She and Paul Methuen had five children; four sons and a daughter.

On 16th March 1658/9 Paul Methuen 'gentleman of Bradford' lent £200 to Robert Earle's son, John Earle now gentleman of Urchfont and his wife Mary on the security of Budbury Farm.[23] The money was to be handed over at the 'now dwelling house of Paul Methuen at Bradford'. Earle was to pay £6 interest on 29th September next, on 26th March 1660 and on 30th September 1660 and repay the £200 plus £6 on 26th March 1661. If he failed Paul Methuen would become the owner.

The mortgage deed describes the property 'now or late' occupied by Robert Earle, father of John Earle, providing us with the list of properties comprising the final third of the combined Ashley and Budbury manors: the capital messuage called Budbury Farm, closes of arable land – Culver Close 3 acres, Wellclose 3 acres, The Park 1½ acres, Upper

Conigree 4 acres, L ower Conigree 2 acres, close of pasture – Davises Grove 4 acres, 5 acres of arable in the common field called Berefield at a place there called Cockstile [north-east of Great Ashley], close of meadow Woodmead [at Forewoods Common] 1½ acres and a meadow in St. Margaret's Moor [south of the town] 1½ acres, closes of pasture – Oakey Leases 8 acres, Little Leys 4 acres, closes of arable - Forestreet 6 acres, Poundmead 4 acres, Oxenleaze 1½ acres.

Part of the agreement but not occupied directly by Robert Earle were; the messuage and closes of pasture called Harvards 14 acres, occupied by William Dunce, messuages and gardens occupied by Richard Hannie, John Harvard, Edward Deverell and Robert Grant. The messuage called the Hermitage with garden and backside 1 acre and two messuages with gardens occupied by Philip Grant.

It is interesting that some of the property was in Bradford well away from both Budbury and Ashley. The loan was not repaid. So in 1661 John Earle the younger of Holt was forced to convey to Paul Methuen, Budbury Farm, the Hermitage and 6 cottages in Newtown tenanted by Richard Hanney, John Harvard, Edward Deverell, Robert Grant, Philip Grant and Robert Shingles. Methuen at the same date bought from Edward Tidcombe three cottages in Newtown tenanted by Thomas Bishop, William Poole and William Jacob, and a piece of common ground measuring 3 rods adjoining Jacob's tenement on the north and the highway on the south in Newtown, waste ground 'with the fountain therein arising'. He also bought from Tidcombe three more cottages occupied by Robert Bollen, Anthony Deverell and William Grant. These leases show that there was a group of small cottages around Lady Well.

One or more stone cisterns were set up at Ladywell by Paul Methuen to make a reservoir of water to serve his house and clothing business at the top of Market Street. Wooden pipes in a stone culvert (which still survives) carried the water to his house with branches serving his properties lower down in Church Street (figs. 19 and 20). In his will written in October 1663 he mentioned the 'cistern that conveys the water to the house and garden'.

After Robert Earle the manor house was no longer occupied as the principal house of a freehold estate. Paul Methuen seems to have converted it to artisan's dwellings. Upper Bearfield Farm in Ashley Road has 17th century features and may have been set up to work some or all of the farmland. It was known as Earls after the former owners of Budbury.[24] The names of the fields when it was sold from the Frankleigh House estate in 1878 clearly link it to Budbury. One was Great Woods of 13 acres and details of the Blanchard daughters' holdings included Budbury Great Wood, a pasture of 9½ acres.

Paul Methuen died in 1667 and probate was awarded to his son John in July that year.[25] His second wife Grace married twice more, becoming Grace Andrews. In January1681 she was living in London. Grace was left Paul's Bradford property except the buildings used in the cloth trade. These were initially used by a nephew of Paul confusingly

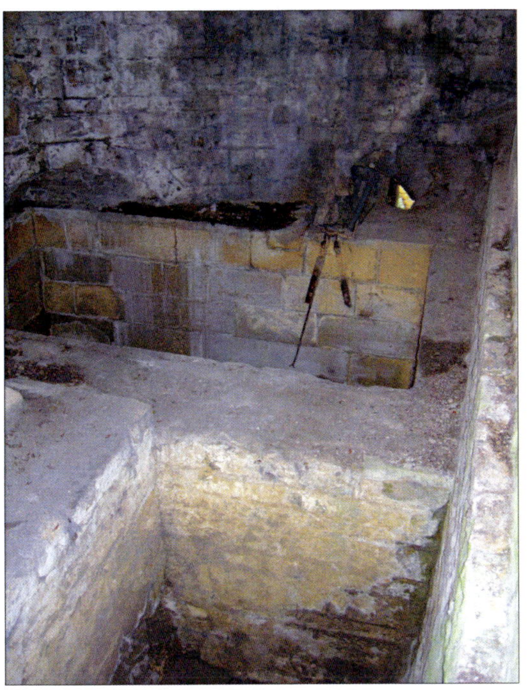

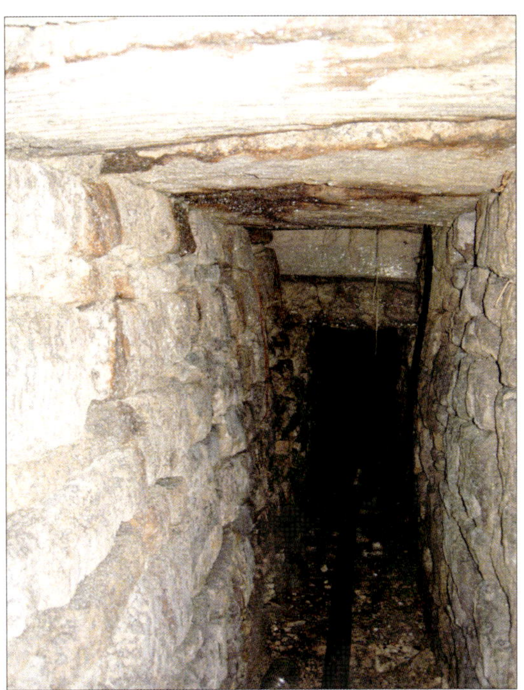

Fig. 19: Cisterns at Ladywell,
facing Newtown

Fig. 20: Conduit with lead pipe and
flagstone ceiling (WBR)

also called Paul Methuen. Their youngest son, Anthony, took over the cloth business after the nephew. His wife was Gertrude Moore of Spargrove, Somerset and she died in 1699, aged 40.

Sale of Budbury land

In August 1671 John, son and heir of Paul Methuen, completed a transaction begun in his father's lifetime.[26] He granted the clothier Anthony Druce a cottage in Bradford, a house and a yard land of 12 acres in Winsley and two fields which had belonged to Budbury Farm; Oake Way of 8 acres (called Oakey Leazes above and likely to be tithe award plot 1182 on the east side of Lower Oakway) and Lytle Lyes of 4 acres (called Little Leys above).

In 1696 Anthony Methuen conveyed to his cousin Paul Methuen five acres of arable land called Pellcombe Park alias Newbury Field situate 'in or near' a field called Berfield.[27] The tithe award shows that 'Belcombe Park' was plots 19, 2029 and 1287, an area between Frankleigh House and Ashley Road, a detached part of Bradford borough. It has no known link with Belcombe by the Turleigh road and the alternative name Newbury is also intriguing.

Development of Newtown and Middle Rank

When John Aubrey wrote about Bradford in the 1660s he commented that the steep hillside of Budbury might be made more profitable.[28] 'This high hill is rock and gravell, faces the south and southwest, therefore is the best seate for a vineyard of any place I know; better in England cannot be'. He also wrote on another occasion of Wiltshire, 'Elders grow everywhere. At Bradford the side of the high hill which faces south, about Mr. Paul Methwin's house, is covered with them. I fancy that that pent might be turned to better profit, for it is situated as well for a vineyard as any place can be, and is on a rocky gravelly ground. The apothecaries well know the use of the berries, and so doe the vintners, who buy vast quantities of them in London, and some doe make no inconsiderable profit by the sale of them.'[29]

Paul Methuen did not exploit the hillside but his son Anthony decided to carry out building development there. He did this at second-hand in the usual way of the time by granting building leases. He laid out three rows of plots on the hillside, now Newtown, Middle Rank and Tory and between 1693 and 1703 a series of leases for 99 years on three lives were granted to local tradesmen, carpenters, masons and weavers, to build on the plots according to his specifications. These mainly controlled the quality rather than the design but they were all built in the prevailing local gabled fashion (fig.21). Each house had to be built of stone and range even with the houses each side. Leaseholders would pay rent and pay for any replacements for 'lives' who died. If the lives ran out or tenants defaulted on the rent, he would regain the houses to lease again.

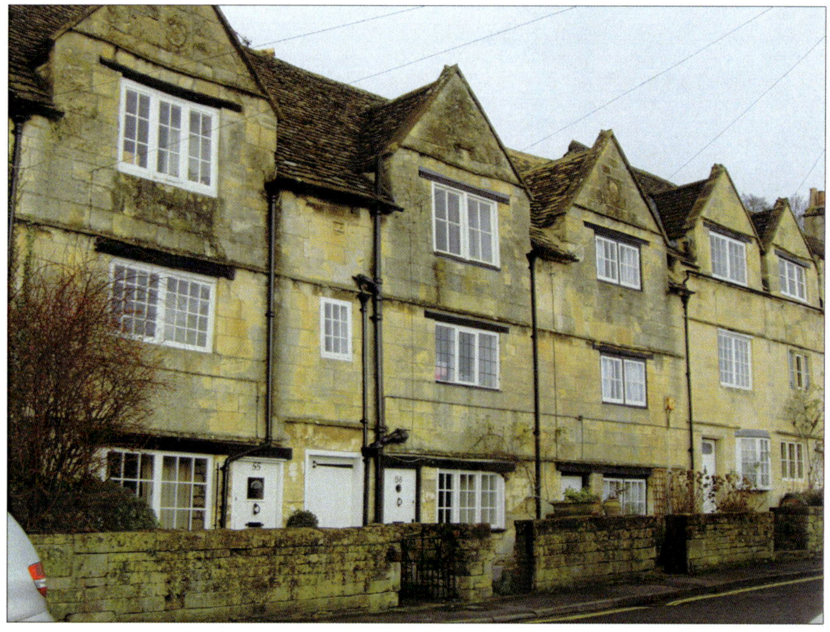

Fig. 21: Newtown (Roger Jones)

The name Newtown at this time seems only to refer to houses around the foot of Wine Street. The south side of the road was in the borough of Bradford. The bottom row of the new houses on the north side of the road was called Lower Rank and its leases began in 1693, followed by the second row called Middle Rank, for which leases were all granted by 1703. A deed of 7.11.1733 recites all the details of the original leases for the Middle Rank and Lower Rank houses.

The plot for the present no. 49 was leased to Henry James, a broad weaver on 10th May 1695.[30] The description is as follows; 'All that plot or parcel of the hilly close of pasture ground of the said Anthony Methuen belonging to Budbury called the Grove in the parish of Bradford in length ranging from the King's Highway on the south side of the said close leading from Newtown to Bradford, upwards towards Budbury aforesaid along by the tenement of Edward Deverell there, as so far to range even with the north end of the gable of the said Edward Deverell and 20 feet in breadth thereof ranging straight from the east side of the said tenement and garden of the said Edward Deverell so far as the 20 feet reacheth. Also free liberty to erect and build against the east poyne end [gable] of the said Edward Deverell's tenement. Rent of six shillings and eight pence for four score and eighteen [98] years. The side walls to be 15 feet high and garden walls 5 feet high.'

Documents suggest there was already one house in the Grove in 1632 and it may have been the present nos. 47 and 48 (see page 32). The roof and other features suggest an early 17th century origin. Edward Deverell who lived there in 1695 came from a family of weavers who had occupied one of the houses by the quarry in Newtown. However, he became a 'rough mason', a builder of rubble walling rather than of ashlar or freestone. In 1698 he took up one of the building leases in Middle Rank above his own house.

Henry James who took up the lease for no. 49 was probably employed by Anthony Methuen, carrying out weaving in his own house, but not all the plots were bought by people in the cloth trade. Some were carpenters or stone masons building for their own use or to sub-let. It seems likely that Henry James employed his neighbour Edward Deverell to build his house. The 20 feet frontage was sufficient for two rooms, probably a larger room with the cooking fireplace at the east end and a smaller room to the west. The entrance was probably in the centre. The 15 feet height provided for two storeys with attic rooms and probably a dormer window or windows in the roof.

Three years later Henry James took up the lease on the plot in the second row immediately behind his garden but 40 feet westwards in width (now probably nos. 13 and 14 Middle Rank). His name is not included in the Poor Rate Book of assessments which started in 1702. The rates of most of the properties were one penny. However, he is on the Methuen Rent Roll of about 1715. His second row property had passed to William Davis by 1732.[31]

The Bell Inn, No. 62 has a datestone for 1695. It was built by Thomas Hillier, carpenter. No. 53 was built by Robert Friend, broad weaver in 1696 and there is a datestone for 1697 on nos. 54-57 built by John Harding, carpenter of Holt. 58 and 59 were built by William Coller, clothworker in 1697 and no. 60 by Robert Turner at the same date. No 61 was leased for 97 years to Richard Smith alias Millard, fuller in 1696. The Grove Meeting House, a Presbyterian chapel, was built in 1698 at the end of Middle Rank (fig. 22). In 1699 a licence for it, described as the 'new erected house of Mr Anthony Methuen' was granted.[32]   52 Newtown, until recently the Masons Arms, was originally built by William Dangerfield, the pastor of the meeting house, for himself.

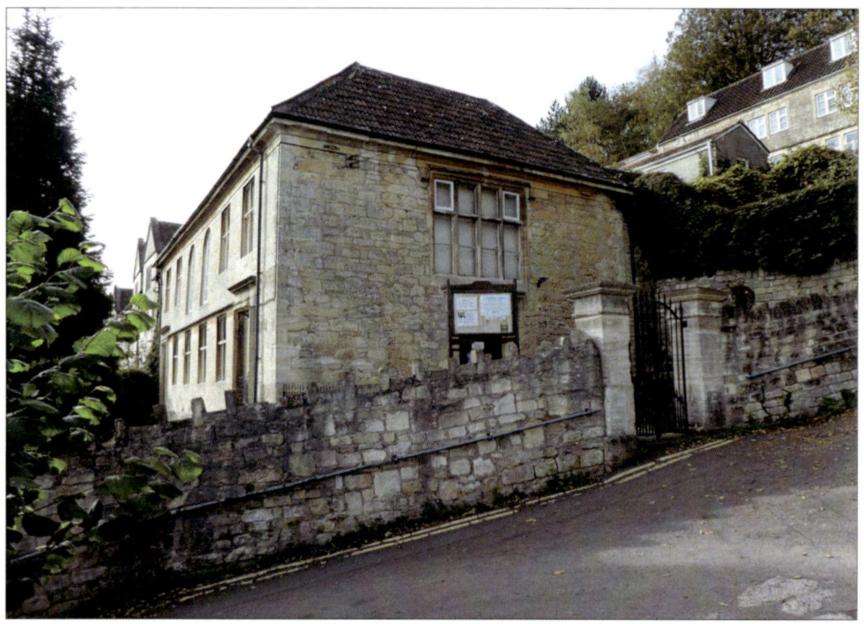

Fig. 22: Grove Chapel from Conigre Hill, now the Zion Baptist Church

Anthony Methuen, clothier

In May 1697 Anthony Methuen, clothier, conveyed his property to trustees for his own use during his life and then for his heirs.[33] It comprised:

> The capital messuage 'wherein he now dwelleth' and all workhouses, shear shops,
> barns, stables, outhouses, gardens, orchards, backsides, ways, waters, conduits,
> pipes and cisterns to the said messuage, the new erected messuage in Bradford
> in the occupation of Alexander Hewis and William Holliday, the messuage in the
> occupation of William Peirce wherein he has an estate for the life of his wife, the
> messuage commonly called Budbury Farm, two grounds called the Conygers, 20
> acres, a close of meadow called Norrises meadow lying near Barton Farm, 6 acres, a
> pasture ground thereto belonging called Well Close, 3 acres, a pasture ground called

the Grove, 3 acres with the several messuages lately new erected and built thereon [Newtown and Middle Rank], a pasture ground called French Grass ground, 6 acres, a pasture ground next adjoining called Hareknapp, 3 acres, a pasture ground called the Park 2 acres, the Hermitage house with a garden and piece of ground thereto belonging, a meadow now in the Moore, 2 acres, a little meadow called Forewoods or Woodmead, 1½ acres. five acres of arable ground in a common field called Burry field near a place called Cocks Style - all in the possession of Anthony Methuen.

It also included messuages tenanted by Francis Yerbury, Matthew Randolph, widow Rogers, Robert Taplin and Edward Harvey and all those several messuages in the several occupations of Edward Deverell junior, John Collett, William Poole, the widow Deverell, Richard Gorton, Robert Rawlings, Anthony Deverell, William Grant and Robert Lacy [the latter were cottages at Lady Well].

There were also two closes of meadow in Ashmeade lately purchased from Christopher Ferris and pieces of arable or pasture in the new 'tyneing' which Methuen had lately made at Hareknapp.

Both the rabbit warrens on the hillside are included in the 20 acres of 'Conygers'; the Little Conigre at Budbury and the Great Conigre to the east, which later became Priory Park.

6 The Eighteenth Century

Methuen Properties

In a survey of 1712,[1] the Budbury farm was described as:

> 'A farmhouse with all houses and outhouses belonging, called Budbury, being stone built, tyled and well timbered adjoining to Bradford. Now converted into seven tenements and in the several tenures of William Batten, Thomas Messiter, William Coombs, David Gore, William Beverstock, Edward White and Edward Say:- £19.5.0 Besides the barns and waine [wagon] house, which are in hand and 40 acres of pasture ground lying round the said farmhouse adjoining to the town: £70.0.'

The farmhouse was well built and the ancillary buildings are likely to have included a dairy and brewhouse. The division of the property into seven tenements may have involved the conversion of the outbuildings, carried out by the Methuen estate since 1661. The estate kept the nearby barton, 'barns and wainhouse' and the 40 acres of pasture, in hand.

The tenants may have worked either in the quarry below or as weavers providing Anthony Methuen with cloth for finishing. Two of the Say family in these trades are recorded. The will of Henry Say, broadweaver of Bearfield, Bradford was proved in 1721 and the estate of Henry Say, mason was administered the following year.[2] The Batten family worked in the same trades at the end of the 18th century. The masons may have worked in Newtown quarry. A 1745 lease of a cottage there reserving the quarry shows it was still used.

In January 1711 Anthony Methuen exchanged with the lord of the manor, the Hon. Francis Powlett, 3 yards of pasture called Palmers Grove in Lower Coniger for 3 yards of pasture called Great French Grass Tyning in Hareknap Field.[3] A yard of land was equivalent to a perch, a fortieth of an acre.

Anthony died in May, 1717, aged 67, and his monument is in Holy Trinity Church. The extensive nature of his trade is shown by the business accounts for the period June 1st 1716 to July 19th 1717, which were drawn up after his death.[4] The outgoings for Spanish wool, drawing designs, pressing cloths, carriage, insurance, Hall and storehouse in London and other things came to £8,557.19s but this was matched by £11,002.3s.1d in hand at the beginning of the period and receipts from 465 cloths sold and the value of 61 cloths unsold 'for Henry Cornish' totalling £18,526.12s.1d. So £9968.13s.1d was passed to his heir. Henry Cornish was a Bradford man, a cloth factor, who went to London rising to become an Alderman and who returned to Bradford in 1683.[5]

Anthony's heir Thomas Methuen took over as a clothier running the family business.

He married Ann Selfe, daughter of Isaac Selfe of Beanacre, Melksham. In 1724 he took up a new lease for 99 years on a house called Gregories from Bradford manor. This may be the messuage or cottage of that name with a barn, garden and orchard which had come to Thomas Allen in the early 17th century as son-in-law of John Blanchard (see page 32). A house of that name in Whiteheads Lane in 1722 was tenanted by Manasseh Whitehead, a Quaker and merchant of the City of London, son-in-law of the Quaker clothier John Collett. The Selfe connection suggests it was Old Manor in Whiteheads Lane which was occupied by Edward Selfe, clothier, (born at Melksham in 1641). His wife was Ann née Hull of Atworth. He died in 1724, the year when Thomas Methuen took up the lease. The name Old Manor has not otherwise been explained but would be applicable if it was indeed the capital messuage of the third part of the combined Ashley and Budbury manors.

It was also in 1724 that Francis Yerbury purchased an acre strip in HareKnap field from the Methuen estate which was the initial plot of Belcombe Court. Thomas died in 1737 and was succeeded by his son Paul. There are portraits of both Anthony and Thomas Methuen at Corsham Court.[6]

A survey of the Methuen Estate Rents was carried out in 1744.[7] The manor house at Budbury appears now to have been in six rented tenements rather than seven.

Budbury: Rents: William Coombs £3, Thomas Messiter £-, Charles Say £-, Samuel
Messiter £-, William Davis £2.10.0, Jacob Say in lieu of Charles £3.

Thomas Messiter and William Coombes were still there though thirty-two years had passed. Samuel Messiter had joined Thomas. Charles Say had replaced Edward Say and in turn had been replaced by Jacob Say. William Davis may be the man whose estate was administered in 1772.[8] He is less likely to have been a 'yeoman' of that name whose will was proved in 1783.[9]

Paul Methuen who succeeded in 1737 had pretensions as a gentleman. He bought Corsham Court in 1745 and the whole family left Bradford in 1763. The Priory was sold to Humphrey Tugwell, clothier. The sale deed refers to 'conduits, pipes, cisterns, watercourses and particularly the whole water leading from the spring head at Newtown to the capital messuage through the lands of Paul Methuen – lead pipes are now placed for conveying the water'. Many of these original lead pipes have survived but some sections have been replaced. Apart from supplying this system, the stream ran to a dipping well south of Newtown, then divided to supply in one direction a conduit house at the west end of Church Street leading to Horton's House and in another the Chantry and Vicarage.

Horton's House, known then as Coombe's, was the other main property of the Methuens. It was sold to the clothier George Bethell in the 1770s with adjoining lands around Abbey Yard. Bethell built Abbey House in 1774 next to Horton's House and diverted the end of Church Street to run alongside the river.[10]

George Bethell

Bethell seems also to have acquired some Methuen farm land. An estate map of Belcombe Court is annotated that lands around the house, purchased since 1777, included, from 'Bethell'; Upper Hareknap 2 acres 3r 22p, Lower Hareknap of 4 acres and Mead of 5 acres.[11] These were strips in the open field which had been amalgamated and enclosed.

In June 1783 a further large number of Methuen properties and land, including parts of Budbury, were sold to George Bethell, now aged 53 for £2,900.[12] In the Western & Midland Directory of that year, he is listed as a 'Superfine Clothier'. (In 1863 the business was insured for £800.)[13] He was also recorded as 'Quarry Master', though the Bethell Quarry off Frome Road, used until recently as a mushroom farm, was developed by a relative in the mid 19th century.

The property and land at Budbury was described as follows:

'And also all those four tenements or dwelling houses with outhouses and gardens thereto belonging situate & being in a certain place called Budbury in the parish of Bradford aforesaid now in the several occupations of Lovel Say, James Bush, James Gurring and George Bull as tenants to the said Paul Methuen and also all that close of pasture ground thereto adjoining called Budbury Barton with the barn, stable and other buildings thereon or some part thereof erected & built and also all that close of pasture ground thereto adjoining called Budbury Park containing by measure two acres and a quarter and also all that close of pasture ground thereto adjoining called the Little Conigre containing by measure twelve acres and a quarter.'

Also sold were Hilly Ground at the south end of Little Conigre, and Great Conigre (on the hillside east of Conigre Lane) comprising 21? acres and 26 perch.

So the tenements at the manor house had been reduced to four. There was still a tenant called Say, as there had been since 1712, whilst the other names had changed.

George Bethell died in March 1795. According to his monument in Holy Trinity Church, he was 'uniformly respected as a man of strict integrity. An upright Magistrate and the poor man's friend.'[14] He was one of four brothers. The eldest, William, had an estate at Beckington, Somerset. Samuel, who died in 1805, had Lady Down Farm between Bradford and Trowbridge. George was the third and the youngest son, Richard, had an inn in Drury Lane, London. George had three daughters.[15] The eldest daughter married the Rev. Bourchier William Wrey in 1789. George Bethell left each of the daughters £15,000. The two younger girls were unmarried, and Ann was to have his gold watch, chain and seals which he wore, while Elizabeth received his best diamond ring. His trustees were to sell his estate to raise money for the legacies.

Bearfield and Huntingdon Street

Bearfield Farm in Ashley Road was once called Earles which links it to the family who had been at Budbury manor (fig.23). It included some outlying Budbury lands including Church Ground, site of the Roman villa. In the early 18th century it was known as Tylers. In 1698 Jonathan Tyler married the widow Katherine, a daughter of Samuel Hull of Frankleigh.[16] Again widowed, she held the farm in 1717. She died in 1726 and the farm went to her son Charles.

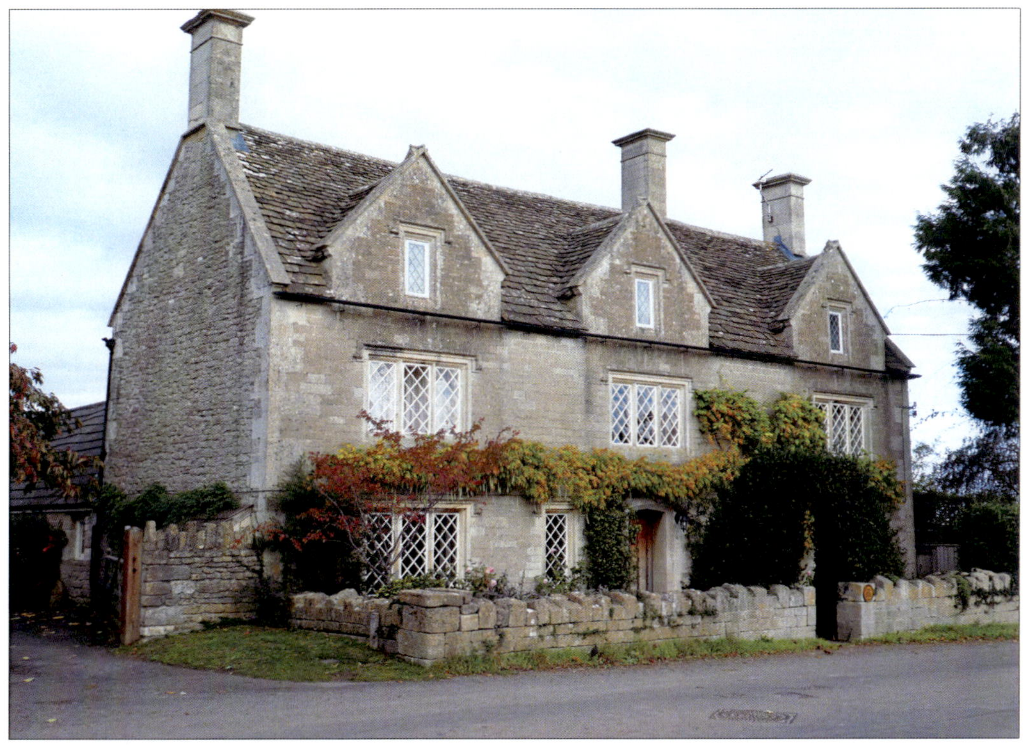

*Fig. 23: Bearfield Farm, Ashley Road, later Upper Bearfield Farm,
now The Old Farmhouse*

The farm with 65 acres was sold in 1743 by Charles Tyler and his wife to William and David Lea at Frankleigh House. The brothers were sons of John Lea of Bradford, gentleman.[17] They bought Frankleigh from the trustees of Joseph Hull in 1746 and the estate included land in both Winsley and Leigh and Woolley tithings. In the years to 1753 they bought more property around Winsley some of which had been part of the Ashley estate. When they partitioned their property in 1753,[18] David had the eastern half which included France Farm at Ashley and Bearfield Farm. These were then farmed together and France Farmhouse became derelict.

At the end of the 17th century, a prosperous period in the town, there was new building in other areas as well as Newtown. Nos. 11 and 12, Huntingdon Street, a gabled house, was built in about 1690 (fig. 24). Nos. 16-18 and 22 are also thought to date from the 17th century.[19] Nos. 13, 14 and 15 stood on a half acre plot and no. 13 incorporates the remains of a fireplace of late 16th or early 17th century date. It was rebuilt in 1774 as recorded on a datestone.

However, much of Bearfield, the common arable field divided by Huntington Street, was still unenclosed in 1705.[20] Nos. 1-5 Huntingdon Street probably date from the early 18th century (fig.25). In 1706 a plot of ground there 'lately enclosed' was leased by John Whatly, to John Scrine of Newtown, broad weaver for 1000 years 'in order to build a tenement'.[21]

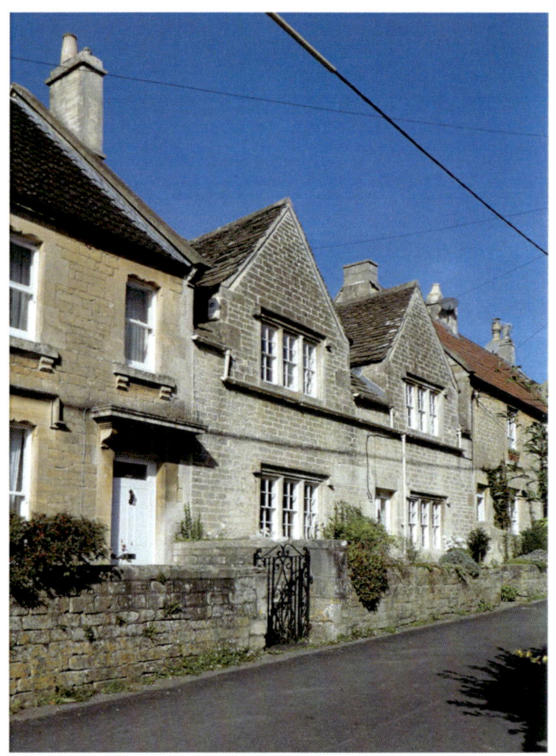

Fig. 24: 12 Huntingdon Street

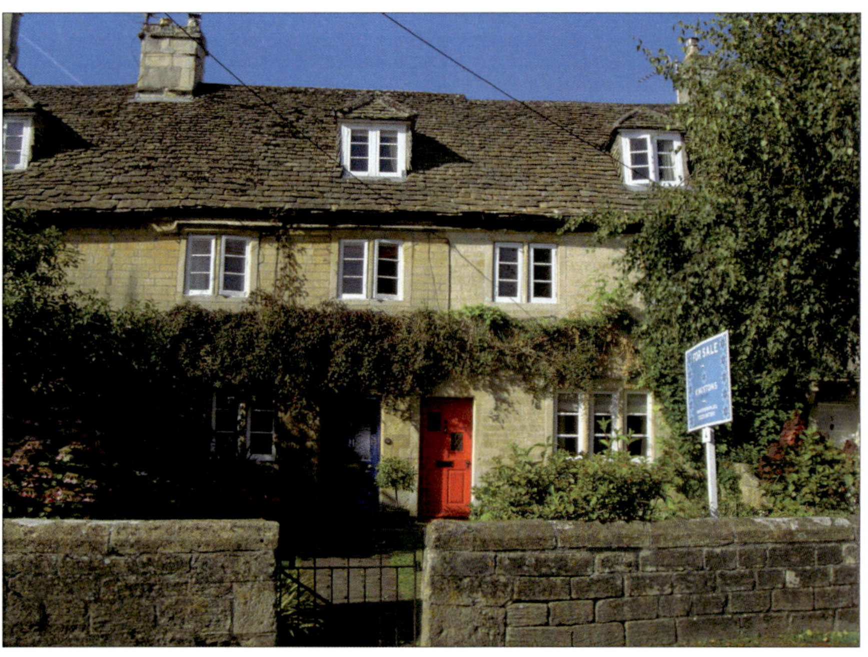

Fig. 25: 3–4 Huntingdon Street

At the northeast corner of Bearfield, where Huntingdon Street meets Ashley Road, the row of houses called Bearfield Rank, now Bearfield Buildings, was developed. Building started at the west end in the mid-18th century on plots laid out by William and David Lea. The lease of the plot for no. 9, not the first, was to Abraham Symes, broadweaver who borrowed £45 from James Lea of Box, mason. In 1750 the plot for no. 11 was also leased to Symes. The lease of the plot for no. 14 in 1757 was from David Lea (who owned it following the partition of the Frankleigh estate) to John Lowther, mason. Lowther's family may have come from Box, as did the Lea family, where extensive quarries occupied many families of masons.[22] Lowther had already built nos. 12 and 13. The next plot, no. 15 was leased on 24th March 1759 to Mary Priest and no. 16 was leased in 1760 again to Lowther.

The next development by John Lowther is of interest. On 26th March 1764, David Lea leased him a close of pasture at 'Budbury' called the Quarr Ground of 1¾ acres.[23] The tithe map shows Quarry Ground was west of Huntingdon Street, on the north side of Winsley Road so this part of Bearfield was considered to be part of Budbury in 1764. The lease for 1,000 years included a covenant to build a good and substantial dwelling house on the plot worth £4 a year. After building these houses at Bearfield, Lowther moved to Walcot, Bath. In 1767 he was said to be late of Bradford and now of Bath.[24] Perhaps John Lowder, Surveyor to the City of Bath 1819-22 was a descendant.

By 1791 the house built on part of Quarr Ground was owned by George Portch, yeoman. In 1799 Portch, described as weaver of Bearfield, made his will. The leasehold house was now described as 'near Budbury 'and occupied by himself, Benjamin Hibbard and his son William Portch. In 1821 Daniel Portch leased Quarry Ground and the house and garden on it to John Bush.[25] In 1878 the property was split into tithe award plots 1188, 1189, 1190, three cottages. To the west was Budbury Tining, plot 1184, previously known as Budbury Field (fig.26). A tyning was a fenced field. This adjoined Church Ground, the site of the Roman villa so the villa site was in an area considered to be Budbury.

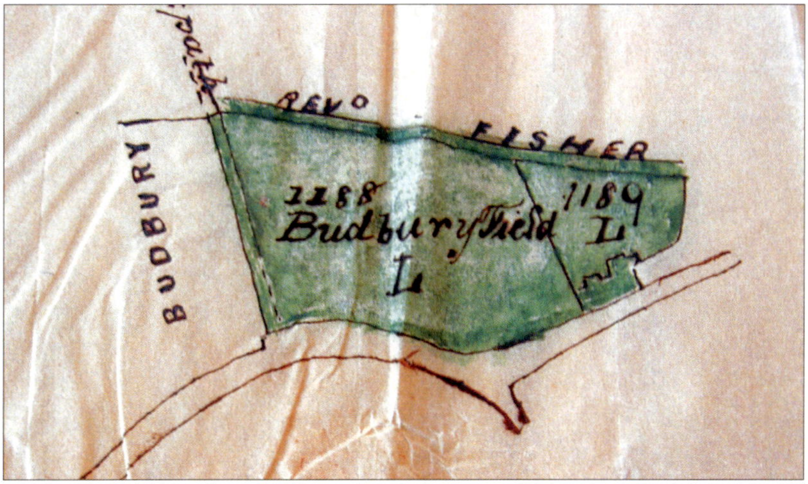

Fig. 26: Budbury Field, later Budbury Tyning, north of Winsley Road with path to Bearfield Farm (WSA)

On the south side of Ashley Road just west of Huntingdon Street, tithe award plot 1273 was the site of another quarry, owned in 1841 by Mrs Ann Richardson, a granddaughter of John Whatley. It was occupied by the builder William Long.

Wine Street

Wine Street was known as Palmer's Lane or Timber Lane. The bottom field on the west side was Sanny's Leaze (now the Sandy Leaze estate) which belonged to Barton Farm and the top field was Coomb's Close. West of these was Hare Knapp common field. In 1724 Edward Thresher at the Chantry leased the land on which No. 13 now stands for 99 years to John Palmer, carpenter, who already had a timber yard there. The lease was on the life of his son Charles Palmer (baptised in 1719).[26] John Palmer's will was proved in 1754. The plot passed through the family and was later owned by John's grandson Richard Smith Palmer, a surgeon.

The development of Tory

Anthony Methuen continued issuing building leases of plots on the hillside. The one which became No. 4 Middle Rank was leased to Edward David of Bradford, clothier in October 1700. The first plot was leased for the 'Third Rank' in about 1695 at the Conigre Hill end. There were further leases in 1706 and 1712.[27] Tory was also known as Top Rank or Upper Rank. In 1743 there were still only five houses at the east end. In 1791 Paul Methuen leased part of the close called the Grove to John Jones, mason, for 99 years and a terrace of six houses was 'afterwards erected on the ground'.[28] In 1796 the executors of George Bethell, with the three Bethell daughters as parties, sold Henry Jones, stone mason, a close called Hilly Close to be used for building.[29] On it he built the terrace nos. 34-37 (fig. 27). He sold no. 34 (now Tory House) in 1805 to James Huntley, a Trowbridge weaver. He

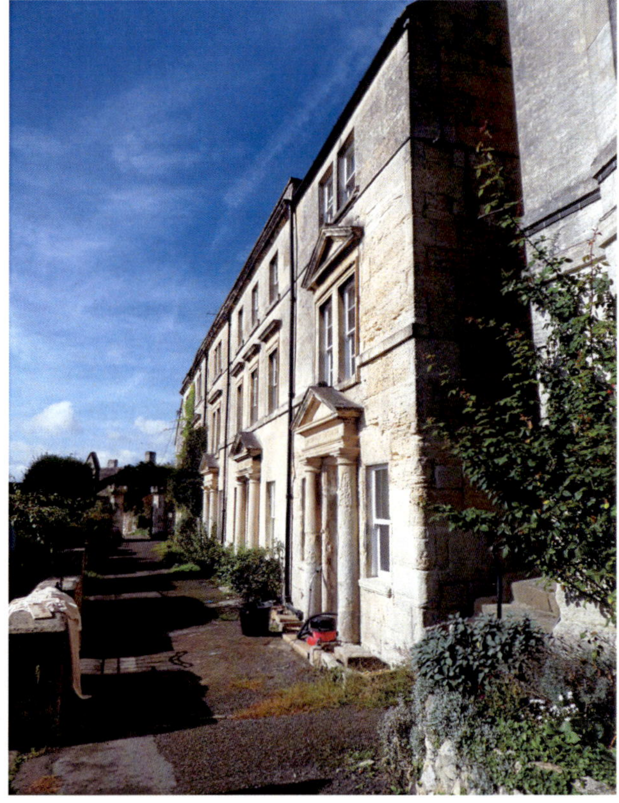

Fig. 27: West end of Tory, no 33 Mountain Cottage and Nos. 34-37 beyond

built Mountain Cottage, 33 Tory, on to the end of the terrace and sold it in 1811. Jones lived at the foot of the hill in a house on the site of Quoins, 32 Newtown.[30] The third rank now straddled the top of Well Path with a flight of steps through as today. The slope of the hill allowed many of the Tory houses to be built as two tenements on top of each other with an upper entrance at the back in Tory Place.

When he made his will in 1807, proved in 1815, Robert Cadby, a builder who came to Bradford in 1785, left to his son Charles no. 36 Tory, purchased from Henry Jones and to his daughter Ann Bulgin a house purchased from Mary Jones and another house in Tory. One of the Tory houses was described as 'lately built' and occupied by Thomas Hayward. [31]

7   The Nineteenth Century

Miss Bethell

The trustees of George Bethell's will did not immediately sell all his estate. One of the two unmarried daughters retained his Budbury property. In 1800 a Miss Bethell was rated 1s 6d for Budbury.[1] The entry for the following year, 1801 has:

> Miss Bethell 1s 2½d, John Jones, mason, part of Miss Bethell's 1d, Henry Jones, part of Miss Bethell's 1d, Joseph Scrine or occupier, part of Miss Bethell's 1½d.

So, probably in 1800, some houses were built on part of the land. Later records suggest that Joseph Scrine was tenant of three which were built on part of Little Conigre and that the ones occupied by the builders and quarrymen, John and Henry Jones, were a semi-detached pair shown on later maps in the grounds of the manor house.

After this the Bethell property was split up and sold. From Easter 1810 Joseph Scrine's property was occupied by three people; Joseph Scrine himself, John Huntley and James Scrine.[2] Each house was valued at ½d rate. In 1815 Joseph Scrine owned and occupied the first house. William Scrine owned the second house with Joseph Scrine occupying it. The houses were now listed as in tithe award plot 24 (taken out of Little Conigre).[3] John Huntly owned and John Spencer (of whom more below) occupied the third house, the former manor house, in tithe award plot 23. The electoral roll of 1818 gives Joseph Scrine as a weaver, entitled to vote as owner of freehold property occupied by himself and another (John Spencer).

Budbury Manor, now 4 Budbury Place

By 1806 the manor house had been bought by Joseph Lasbury, broad weaver.[4] On June 6th that year he sold it to on to Emanuel Baily, baker. The building was described as a dwelling house with a garden in the front and on the west side. Emanuel Baily then bought the New Bear Inn in Silver Street in 1810 from John Deverell of Frankley for £1,042, with a mortgage of £800. He soon defaulted on payment of the mortgage interest and was forced in 1811 to sell both the house at Budbury and the inn to Hosier Saunders and John Spencer, as trustees, to settle his debt. The deed gives William Beasor as the tenant of the manor house.

John Spencer came from Little Chalfield where the family lived in the second half of the 18th century. He was baptised at Great Chalfield in 1763, the first son of Thomas and Hannah Spencer. Thomas was a yeoman who died in 1802. John, as the eldest son, was set up in farming as leaseholder of Barton Farm at Bradford in 1796 but also went into brewing.[5] He is listed as a common brewer in Whitehead's Lane in 1822 (behind the New Bear Inn) and John Spencer & Co were listed as brewers in Silver Street by

1830.[6] Their brewery and the Newtown Brewery became the most prominent breweries in the town.

Two months after the mortgage default, in December 1811, Hosier Saunders and John Spencer sold the two properties to John's younger brother Walter who had inherited Little Chalfield manor. In 1817 he sold them back to John in trust for the use of John Hazeland, brewer, for life and after to John Spencer's heirs. Hazeland had married John's sister Elizabeth Spencer in 1785. In 1815, we have seen that John Spencer was already using the manor house (perhaps for an employee) as sub-tenant of John Huntley, the tenant who paid the Church Rate.

In 1820 Thomas Earl paid the Poor Rate as tenant. In the Poor Rate of 1834 the house is assessed as two times ¼d and so had been converted into two tenements. After John Spencer's death in 1837, the 1837-8 Rate Book names the two tenants: James Davis, occupying the slightly larger part and William Bowles the other part. According to the 1841 census James Davis was a labourer about 40 years old. Living with him were his wife Sarah aged 29 and children George 20, John 19, Daniel 18, Annie 12, William 8, James 5 and Thomas 1 year.

In October 1840, John Spencer's sons, Walter and John, sold the house for £50 to Thomas Smart, corn factor and George Smart, grocer.[7] John Hazeland who had the 'use' of the building for life had been buried at Devizes on 20th January 1832. Thomas Smart was a baker, grocer and tea dealer in 1830.[8] He built Bradford's windmill, 4 Mason's Lane. He bought the land in the early 1800s, erected the mill and in about 1809 advertised for help. The venture failed and in March 1813 the mill was for sale 'quite new' with all or any part of the interior works.[9] It was then converted into two tenements. Thomas Smart's shop was at 35 Market Street and George Smart was a wholesaler in Mill Street.[10]

In 1840 James Dix had replaced William Bowles as one of the occupants of Budbury Manor. In 1841 his widow Mary, aged 55, was a clothworker.[11] The head of the family was now Samuel Dix aged 35, labourer and there were five children in the tenement. The property was described as 'All that tenement or dwelling house with the garden in the front and west side thereof, being at Budbury, bounded on the south east by a road or way dividing the same from a field called the Conigre, and on all the other sides thereof by a field called the Park, by a garden late of John Jones, mason, and by Budbury Barton which said messuage or tenement has been converted into two dwelling houses.' The former park, tithe award plot 21, was in use as pasture in 1841.

Thomas Smart died in December/ January 1844-1845 leaving everything to his wife Ann. In 1849 she sold the house at Budbury for £35 to the plasterer and tiler Thomas Webb. The tenants were James Davis and now William Cooper. In 1857 Webb defaulted on a £45 mortgage he had taken from the brewer Alexander Wilkins. He was now also described as 'innkeeper' because he was the brewer and licensee of the Bell Inn in Newtown.[12] The Budbury house and all Webb's other possessions were assigned to Wilkins and to Thomas Taylor, chemist, druggist, wine and spirit merchant at 14 Silver Street, to whom Webb probably owed money for stock.

The house was auctioned at the Seven Stars public house in Newtown on 12th November 1857. The buyer was Charles Humphries paying £55. The conveyance is dated a little later, on 4th May 1858, and Humphries is described as of Bearfield, yeoman. He was perhaps the tenant of Upper Bearfield Farm but also an investor in property. He died in 1877 and his will mentions houses at Barton Orchard and Lady Well bought from John Gifford, houses in Middle Rank bought from Joseph Gordon Jones, houses at Budbury bought from John Bush and houses at Bath Road 'lately erected by me'. Budbury Manor remained in his family until 1929.

The Jones family of builders and quarrymen

In 1808 John Jones, brother of Henry Jones, owned nos. 2-8 Middle Rank, a plot first leased for building in 1700, and now perhaps used to house his workers. He built nos. 25-32 Tory between 1805 and about 1812 (fig. 28). John and Ann Jones (who died in 1814 and 1836) had three sons, Daniel, Charles and Brian. Daniel went to London, became bankrupt and returned to Bradford where he worked a quarry with a brother, probably Charles.[13] Daniel and Charles built Christchurch in 1841 to cater for the top of the town. Brian was tragically killed in 1843.[14] He was the contractor for the new Romanesque-style church at Wilton and fell 28 feet from the roof, dying of internal injuries. As he regularly employed 400 workmen, most of the town attended his funeral. After Charles died in 1852, Daniel carried on the firm alone and died in 1866. The architect T. H. Wyatt said they worked with him for 25 years without one misunderstanding on the

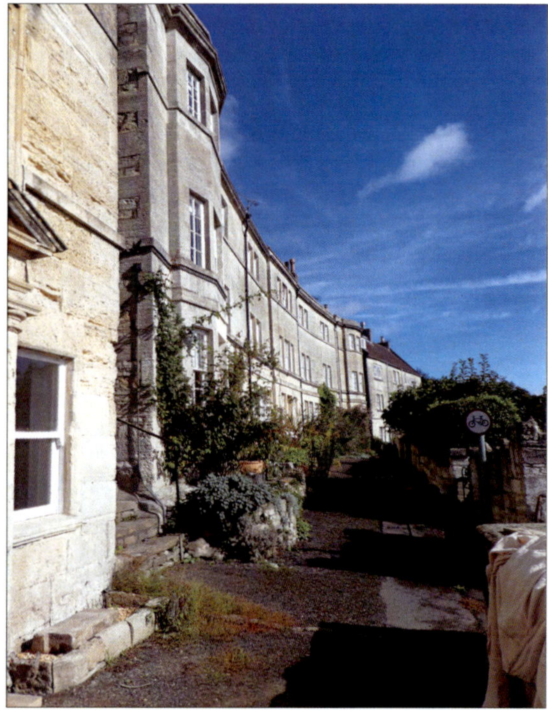

Fig. 28: Curved terrace built by John Jones, 26-32 Tory

estates of the Duke of Beaufort, Lords Lansdowne, Ailesbury, Bath and Pembroke and they built or restored 18 churches.[15] John Jones, of a younger generation, lived in Wine Street in 1822.[16] A stone mason of the same name was living in the house on the site of 32, Newtown in 1852-3, previously occupied by Henry Jones.[17]

In 1853 when a house and garden in Tory were conveyed by a trustee of Lord Methuen to the brewer Alexander Wilkins, the conveyance referred to six cottages lately built by John Jones.[18]

The pair of houses in the grounds of Budbury Manor

A property on the Bethell land in the curtilage of the manor house is no longer there. It was tenanted by John and Henry Jones in 1801 who perhaps built it. It was then bought from the Bethell estate freehold by John Saunders the younger of Bradford, clothier. His father, John Saunders senior, a collar maker, had purchased the former Methuen house (The Priory) in 1811 and died in 1816. John junior sold the Budbury property to Peter Wheeler.[19] It was described as a messuage or tenement with a court and garden in front on the south-west side and the field called the Park on the north. It had been formerly in the occupation of Joseph Evans, since James Bricker, afterwards of Edward Rickets and now of John Rickets. John Rickets occupied the house for a long period and was still there is 1837/8.

Peter Wheeler, the buyer of the house, already owned the freehold of the Mason's Arms in Newtown and was listed as a baker, grocer and tea dealer in 1822 and a baker in 1830.[20] His wife was Margaret Batten, presumably from the local family of builders. She died in July 1834, 'of Newtown', and Peter was buried at Holy Trinity on 10th September that year. In 1833 Peter Wheeler passed property including some at Tory and this at Budbury 'with love and affection' to his son and heir Thomas.[21]

Thomas Wheeler was born at Exeter but baptised at Holy Trinity, Bradford in 1783.[22] He was a corn dealer in Newtown in 1822.[23] He is later recorded as a baker and, later still, a prosperous maltster. He inherited other property from his father and purchased other Bethell land at Budbury. He was elected a Town Commissioner in 1839. In 1842 he bought the leasehold of Church House in Church Street, which was partly used as a bank.[24] He died in 1870.

In 1840 the garden of the pair of houses was said to be 'late of John Jones'. The houses are shown on the tithe map of 1841 as plot 22A, facing south (fig. 29). On the 1864 map the west house is larger than the east house and has a small outbuilding attached on the west side. Both houses have an attached building behind, possibly a wash-house. On the O.S. map of 1887 the building is in four occupations with a path to Budbury Manor and towards a small building, possibly a pigsty, in the corner of the manor house garden. On the 1899 map there is a new extension behind the two tenements at the west end.

Budbury Barton

In 1806 the manor house plot was described as 'bounded by' Budbury Barton, showing that the farmyard had also been sold out of the Bethell estate. It had formerly been

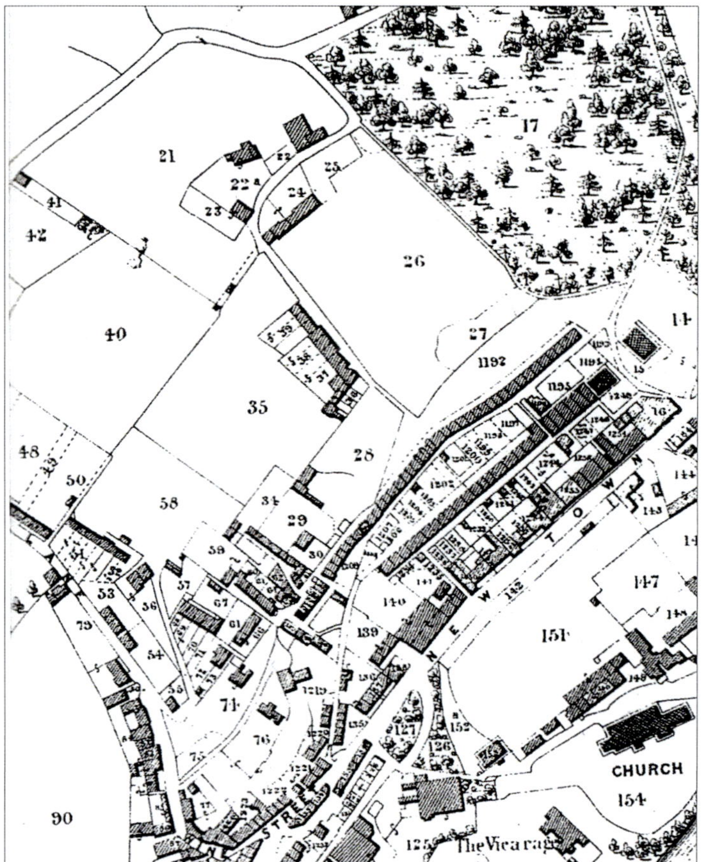

Fig. 29: Tithe map, 1841
Plot 23 Budbury Manor,
plot 21 The Park,
plot 22 Budbury Barton,
plot 26 Little Conigre

within a triangular plot including the manor house. By this time the east part of the buildings was converted into a house. A fireplace, and a south porch, shown on drawings but now gone, date from around 1800. A former wagon entrance arch at the east end is older. The Barton, tithe award plot 22, was owned in 1841 by Thomas Wheeler and occupied by Samuel Hiscox. The 1864 map shows the east end of the buildings coloured pink, indicating domestic use. Job Knight was the farmer at Budbury in 1890 and probably lived there.[25]

Little Conigre

Thomas Wheeler sold on some of his Budbury property. In a deed of 1818 he was described as having sold 7 acres 17 perches of land to James Bulgin and a similar piece of land to John Jones of Bradford, mason. An 1821 deed concerns allotment land and a cottage at Budbury, comprising 16 perches, part of a close called Little Conigre. Little Conigre (tithe plot 26), the field east of Budbury Manor, was shown with three small plots taken from the north end, the divided plot 24 with houses and plot 25 empty. The land which was sold in 1821 was bounded on the east by a road leading to lands formerly owned by John Jones and others (shown as a lane on the tithe map leading to a quarry and on to join Conigre Hill) and on the south by the rest of Little Conigre. It was conveyed in 1821 by James Bulgin to Messrs John Randell, Henry Challenger, John Price, mason and William Merrick, gent. Bulgin was a brother-in-law of the Cadby family of builders.[26] He was a baker in Church Street in 1822. A mortgage of the same property in 1885 describes it as having Little Conigre also on the north and west which is difficult to reconcile. By then three tenements, erected on the land, were called 4, 5, and 6 Budbury Place. In 1864 the remaining semi-detached pair were in ruins. By 1901 only the house on the corner remained.[27]

Quarries

The demand for stone resulted in surface quarrying on top of the hill. Three quarries are shown on maps. One is marked in 1885 in the northwest corner of Budbury. Bert Niblett described it in 1981 as in the garden of Alpine Cottage, (formerly Prospect Cottage) at the top of Wine Street on the east side 'almost under the ground'.[28] It now contains an electricity sub-station. Another is shown in 1885 at the southwest corner of the hillfort and now in Budbury Close. Bert Niblett described it as at Wine Street Terrace in the garden of a bungalow. An underground working opened from an arch in the garden and continues into a deep fissure in the rocks called a 'gull' caused by geological movement along the edge of the hillside.[29] The fissure was named Gorton's Rift after a former owner of the house. A blocked shaft once reached the surface. The third is at the bottom east part of Little Conigre, marked as plot 27 on the 1841 tithe map and called 'Old Quarry' on the O.S. map of 1885. It had probably been worked by John Jones but was used as a garden by Thomas Wheeler in 1841. Bert Niblett[30] said 'At Budbury, there are quarries in the garden of Budbury Cottage, which extend under a field that I remember being called "Bed and Bolster", now a paddock.' The house, 9 Budbury Place, was formerly called Badgers and the paddock on the north side was Little Conigre. The underground working was entered by a slope shaft from the open quarry in the cottage's garden. Canon Jones, writing in the 1850s, said that the field had signs of earthworks, 'and these, a few years ago, were distinctly traceable in some of the adjoining pieces of ground, before they were portioned off as garden-plots, and then levelled.'[31] He thought the local name 'Bed and Bolster' referred to 'the "vallum" and its corresponding "agger" in a Roman encampment.' It now seems more likely these were the remains of the pillow mounds of the rabbit warren.

Most of the southern edge of Budbury has evidence of quarrying and the three ranks of housing had required terracing which must have produced building stone. At the top the good stone was followed into the hill by tunnelling. Behind Tory the Jones family had three or four entrances or adits, including a blocked one in the garden of 19 Tory (fig. 30). When its roof fell in a stone was seen inscribed 1814.[32]

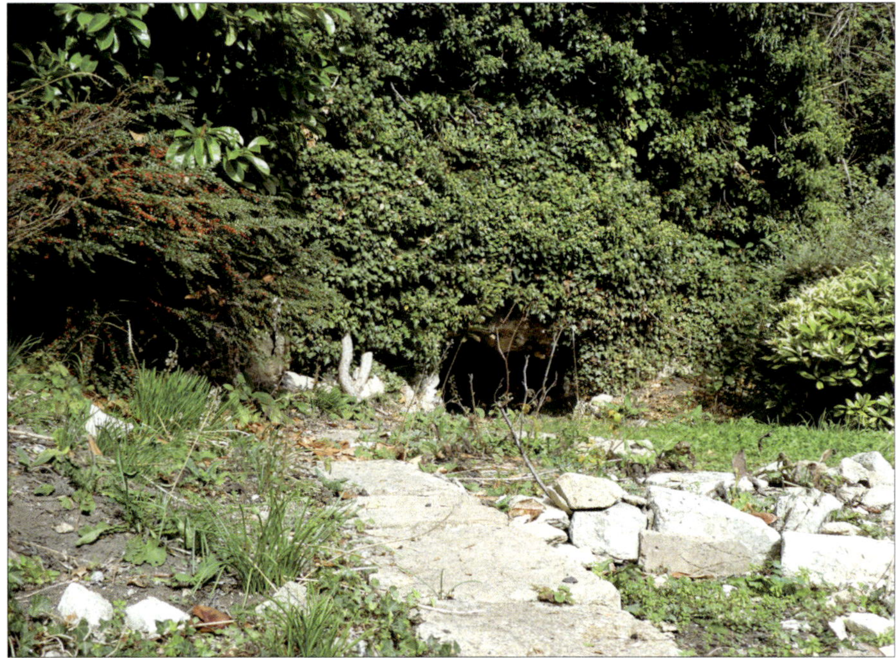

Fig. 30: Quarry entrance behind 19 Tory

Budbury Castle

A tall Italianate tower was built on the south side of Winsley Road and is first mentioned in the Church Rate Book of 1837/8 (fig. 31a and b).[33] It was plot 44 on the tithe map in 1841 owned by Thomas Wheeler, maltster and occupied by Richard Gardiner who also occupied the houses and garden at plot 43 on the east side. It is likely to have been built by Wheeler. The Church Rate Book of 1837/8 lists the next building after Richard Gardener's house and Budbury Castle as a house owned by Wheeler and occupied by James Scrine. This was part of TA plot 24, former Bethel property.

George Ashmead's 1837 plan of the town labels the tower Budbury Castle and shows it in grey as uninhabited. It was presumably a folly, an unoccupied observation tower. Photographs show it had four storeys with a lower castellated addition. The lower part was added in 1850 according to a plaque, after which time it was inhabited. In 1851 the head of the family there was Henry Neate, florist and seedsman, born at Freshford. By 1864 the Castle was owned by Thomas Wilkins, a coal merchant and the tenant was James Bagg. In 1876 Thomas Bush Saunders of the Priory bought the Castle from Eliza Wilkins, widow. The 1885 O.S. map calls the building Budbury Villa though by 1891 the original name was restored. It was said in 1939 to have been part of the old Priory estate and in an excellent state of preservation with both inside and outside staircases.[34] It was demolished in the 1960s and nos. 58, 59 and 60 Winsley Road were built on the site.

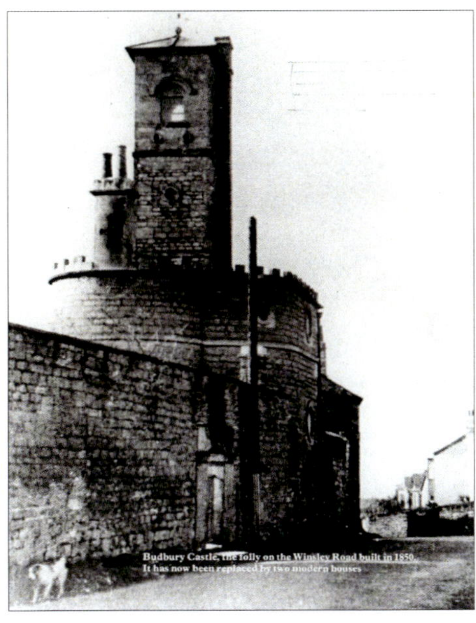

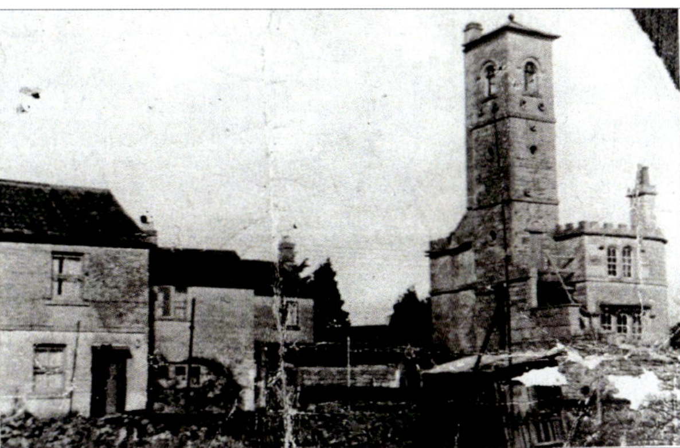

*Left, Fig. 31a: Budbury Castle from
Winsley Road (WCC)*

Above, Fig. 31b: Budbury Castle from south

Rev. John Skinner's visit

The antiquarian, the Rev. John Skinner of Camerton, Somerset (1772-1839), visited Bradford in October 1819 and sketched various places and relics of historical interest.[35] His sketch of Budbury, which he calls 'British Settlement above Bradford', (fig. 4) is a view across Wine Street from Sandy Leaze and shows a group of houses at the top which may be nos. 65-68 Winsley Road, on the top corner of Wine Street. They face south and No 68, Rowan Cottage, has a stone band at first floor level suggesting an early 19th century date. Skinner shows various archaeological features on the hill; 'graves' indicated by circles above Tory, 'vallum' above Wine Street and he labels Wine Street 'Road from [Winsley?]'. Two old graves have been discovered in recent years in Budbury Close.

The roads at Budbury

Winsley Road from Wine Street to Bath Road was known as Budbury Lane in 1820.[36] (From Wine Street to Winsley it was called Oakway and the fields each side had the same name.) The houses of the town were numbered by the Town Commissioners in 1882 for the first time.[37] They said Budbury Lane, 'now called Church Lane', (as Christchurch had been built since 1820), was in future to be called Winsley Road.

It is suggested above that the road across the top of Budbury may have originally passed on the west side of Budbury Manor (fig. 7). It could have been diverted when the park was made next to the house. The Ordnance Survey First edition of 1817 shows a sickle-shaped road in the hillfort. The 'handle' is a continuation of Wellpath and it curls round in a semi-circle to the manor house and in front of the barton. The tithe map shows the road in a similar position (fig. 29). The dogleg at the Barton was formed by the track from Wellpath meeting the lane coming straight up from Conigre Hill past a quarry.

The line of the road was then altered to the present position from the manor house direct to Winsley Road (fig. 32). On 9th August 1870 The Town Commissioners agreed to allow T.B. Saunders to widen the footway 'near Mrs Janes's house' at Budbury to be the width of the road above and to alter 'the other footway and roadway at Budbury'.[38] It was to come out opposite 'the existing footway leading to Church Ground' (site of the Roman Villa) and Upper Bearfield Farm. These new roads replaced the existing ways leading from the back of Sion Chapel (at the end of Middle Rank) to Budbury Lane (Winsley Road) and from Budbury Lane back to Budbury Well (near Budbury manor).

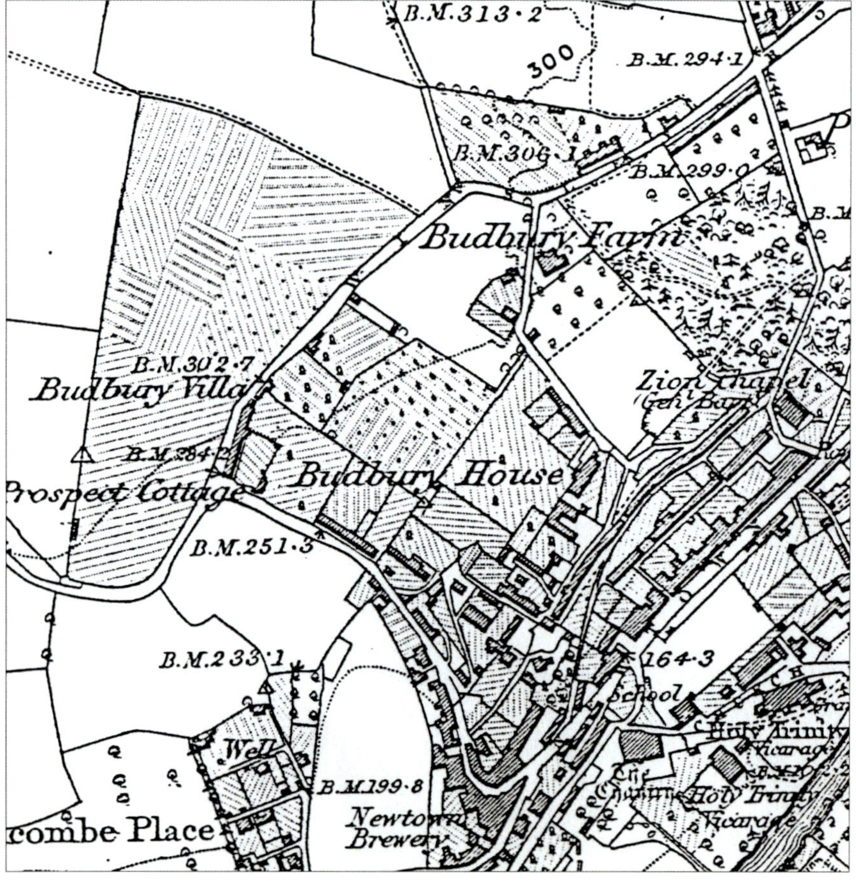

Fig. 32:
O.S. 1886

Houses in Winsley Road

No. 54 was demolished in 2018 (fig. 33). It was originally called Budbury Park Cottage and was built in about 1830 facing south with its back to the road. It was three storeys tall at the front to take advantage of the view. In 1841 it was owned by the representatives of John Bains and in 1864 by T. B. Saunders with two tenants.

The row of eight houses, nos. 31-38 also faces south (fig. 34). They are on the west side of the intersection where Conigre Hill and Huntingdon Street cross Winsley Road. In 1841 they were owned by Thomas Hosier Saunders of the Priory, a J.P. and clothier and occupied by tenants of Thomas Wheeler. In 1864 they were called Conigre Rank and owned by his son Thomas Bush Saunders. Below the houses is an area called the Wilderness which was at one time a garden feature in the grounds of the Priory.

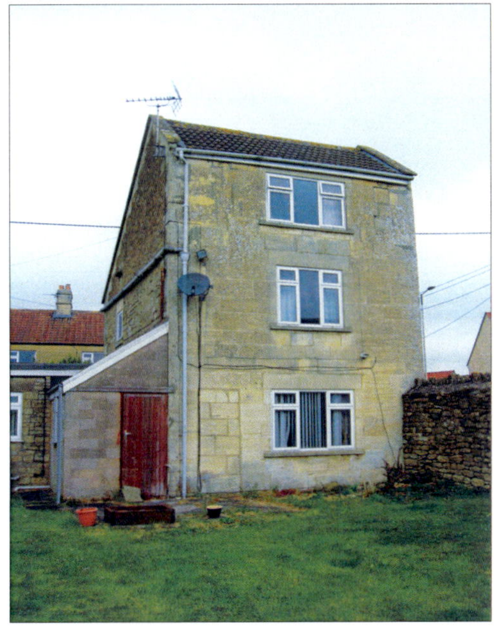

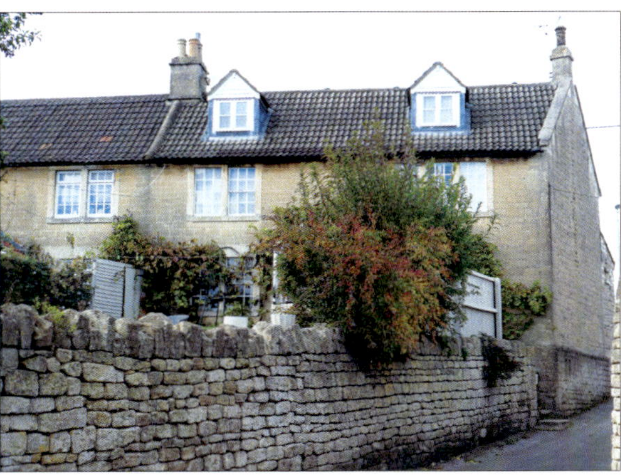

Left, Fig. 33: Budbury Park Cottage, 54 Winsley Road, 2018

Above, Fig. 34: 31-38 Winsley Road from Conigre Hill

Huntingdon Street

The community here developed its own facilities. Bethel Chapel was built on the east side of the street in 1787.[39] It was originally Independent but in the early 19th century became attached to the Countess of Huntingdon Connection, an offshoot of the Methodists. Providence Baptist Chapel opened in Bearfield Buildings in 1858. Nos. 3 and 4 Huntingdon Street was a public house in 1834/5. When in 1882 the Town Commissioners were numbering the houses they decided to start with No. 1 'being the baker's shop'.

Wine Street

The name of the road, Palmer's Lane or Timber Lane in the 18th century, began to change in the 19th century. Its name is unlikely to have any connection with wine. An 1822 reference has Wind Street.[40] Ashmead's map of 1837 labels it Wine Street at the foot and Palmer's Lane at the top. The name probably refers to how it winds around at the bottom. 'Wine' is dialect for 'wind'. The tithe map and the survey accompanying Ashmead's 1864 map revert to calling it Palmer's Lane.

The Newtown brewery incorporates, at the west end, a former cloth factory. In 1812 Thomas Timbrell conveyed to George England, a clothier, several houses and a factory or workshop in Newtown.[41] England took out a mortgage from Timbrell. England's will was proved in 1814.[42] The four-storey clothing workshop at the foot of Wine Street backed onto the quarry face. In 1822 it belonged to Mr England and a room adjoining it was registered as an Independent chapel.[43] In 1835 two tenements in Wine Street, the workshop adjoining 'lately used in the clothing business' and three other tenements and another messuage in Wine Street were advertised for sale (fig. 35).[44] England's house, which has a forecourt, is at the foot of the street on the west side, now 4, 6 and 7 Wine Street (fig. 36a and b).

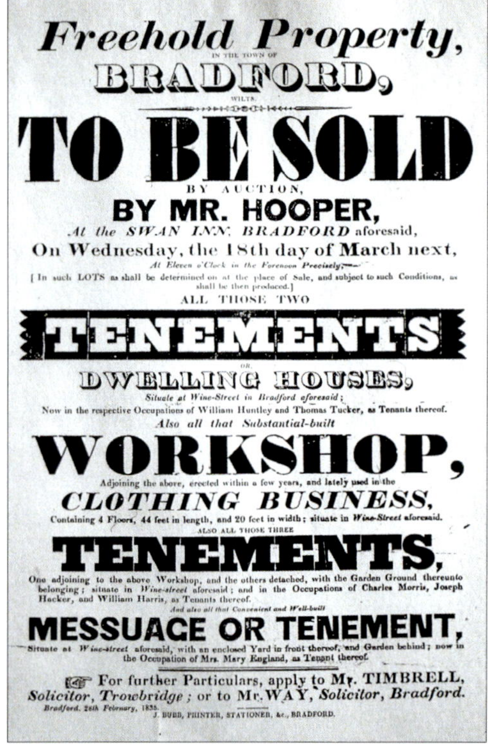

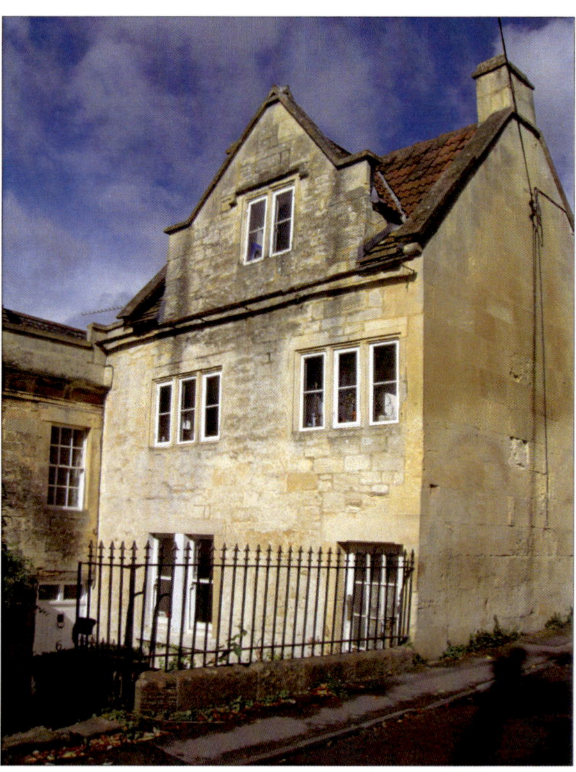

Above left, Fig. 35: Sale advertisement for the workshop building (WSA)

Above right, Fig. 36a: 6 Wine Street

A row of tenements called Cadby Buildings was constructed further up on the east side of the street by the builder Charles Cadby in the 1820s (fig. 37). They were four storeys high to make full use of the narrow site. From the middle of the row steps led up to a pump at the back. They were demolished at some time in 1958 having become very run down.[45]

Prospect Cottage, 22 Wine Street, at the top on the Budbury hill side is shown on the

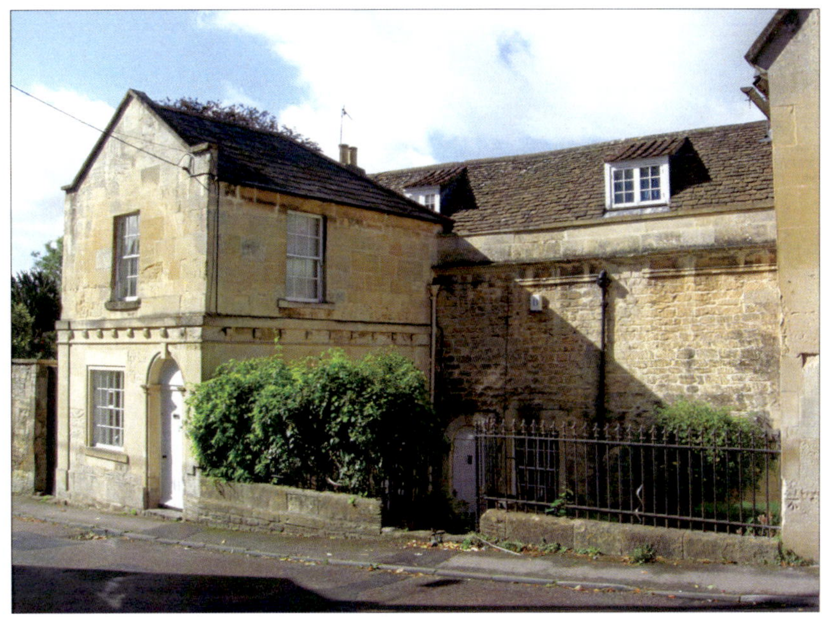

Fig. 36b: George England's house in Wine Street

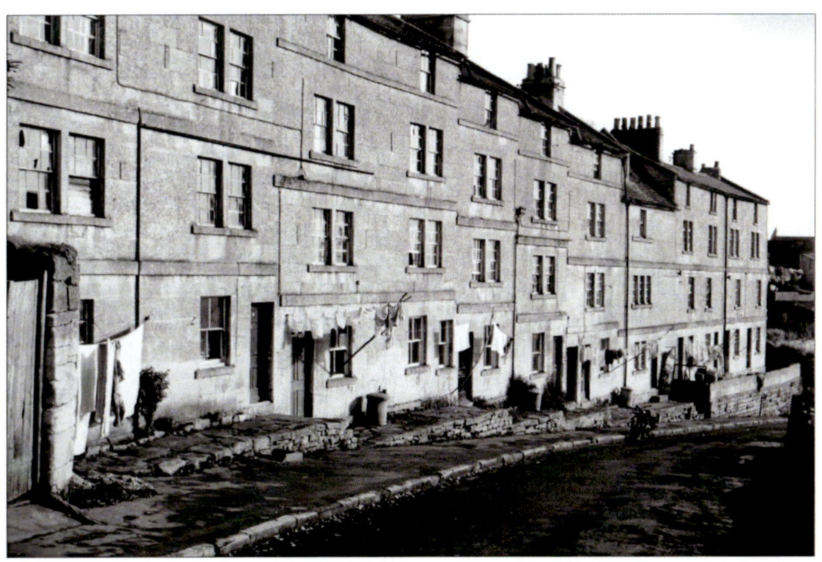

Fig. 37: Cadby Buildings in Wine Street, 1956 (Geoffrey Wright)

1837 map. Rose Cottage, 12 Wine Street, on the west side of the road, was erected by Richard Carpenter in 1822. His own house was in St. Margaret's Street. His tenant in 1824 was William Hillman, a baker. The site of no. 13 was land which Edward Thresher at the Chantry sold to John Palmer in 1724. It was sold in 1820 by William Heal to George Grist, a carpenter. By 1876 both 12 and 13 belonged to the artist Mrs Elizabeth Tackle, then a widow, and they were described as two houses, a baker's shop and a garden.

Triphony, 35 Wine Street, has a triangular plan of three storeys to fit into a small plot next to a short lane running diagonally up to the quarry site on the hilltop (fig. 38). It looks Italianate and was built between 1841 and 1864 when it was in four tenements. On the other side of this lane are Vine Cottages, shown as six houses in 1887 and now two.

The houses of Wine Street Terrace are perched on the edge of the hill overlooking Wine Street, from where they are reached by a pathway. There is also a path from Tory Place at the rear. They are constructed of stone with stone bands at storey height and are likely to date from the 1820s or 30s. No. 12 is separate and southwest of St. Mary Tory.

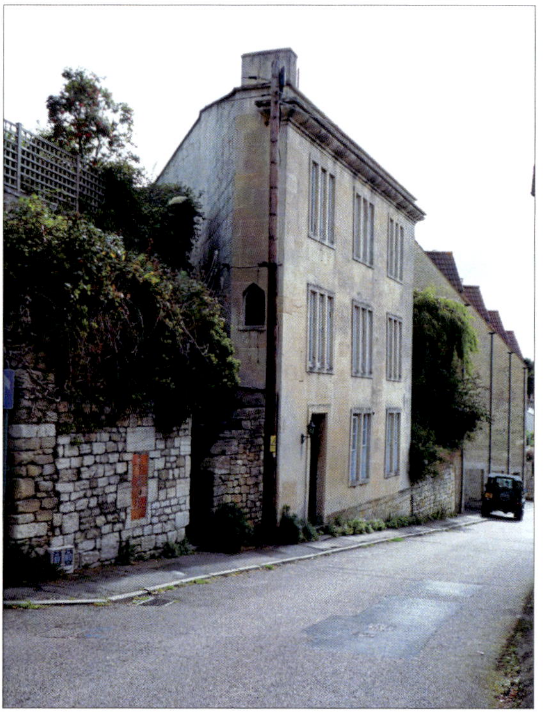

Fig. 38: Triphony, Wine Street

Bearfield Farm in Ashley Road and Budbury fields

On 11th February 1813 'Berfield' Farm, one mile from Bradford, was advertised to let with a good dwelling house and 22 acres of arable and 78 acres of pasture.[46] It was sold out of the Frankleigh House estate in 1878.[47] Its farm buildings, a barn, wheelhouse, cart house, granary, cow stall, stable and cow house, were across the road in part of what had been the open field. Its land, now totalling 82 acres and 39 perches, included some that had belonged to France Farm at Ashley. It had probably all been within the combined Ashley and Budbury manors (fig. 39). One block of four arable fields comprising just over 39 acres were in a single close in 1878 and two had Budbury Ley names. On the tithe map of 1841 they are plots 1178, 1179, 1309 and 1311. Ley or leaze indicates a pasture. The farm also had Great Woods, the former Budbury wood next to the site of the Roman villa.

Rebuilding of the Hermitage

By 1841 the building had become a 'house and garden' owned by James Marks and occupied by Thomas Bigwood, the plumber, who may have used it for an employee.[48] The chapel part was ruined. In 1842 W.C. Lukis, curate at Holy Trinity, drew a plan of the chapel and a scale drawing of the statue niche in the southeast corner.[49]

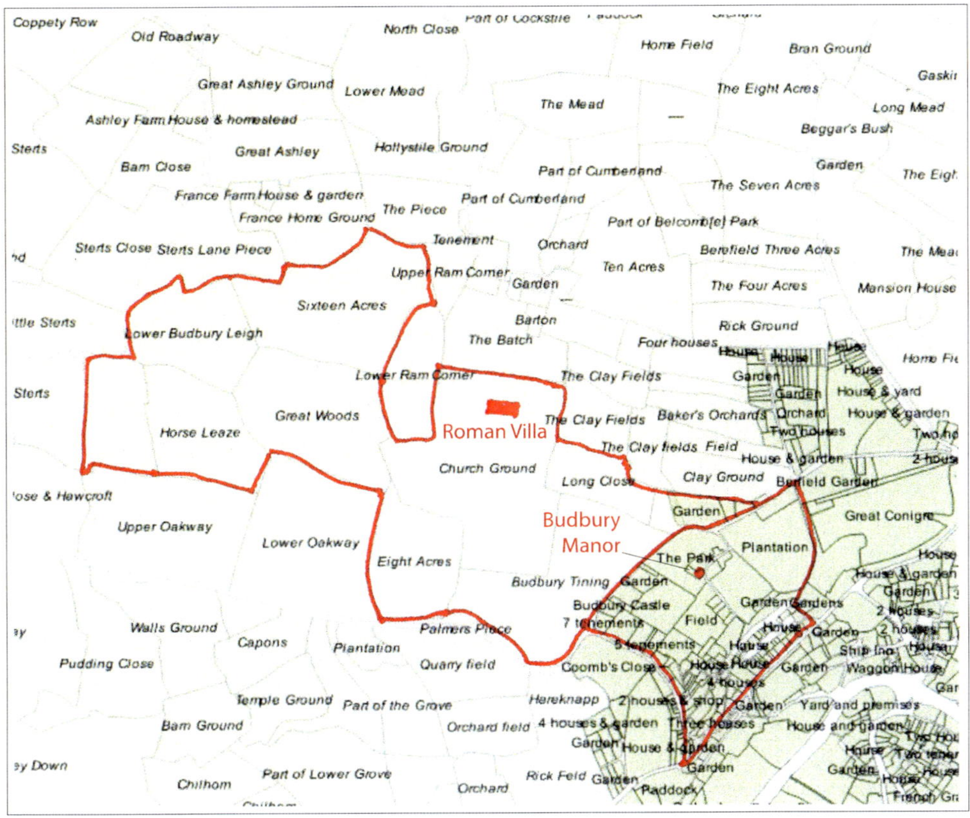

Fig. 39: Budbury fields

In July 1846 the Hermitage, called 'Tory House, formerly known as the Old Roman Chapel', tenanted by James Bricker, was for sale along with three houses in Newtown at the foot of Wine Street, four houses at Ladywell opposite and a substantial house with a walled garden and brewhouse in Barton Orchard tenanted by Mrs Shrapnell.[50] It was described as commanding 'not only a view of the town, but the surrounding country for many miles. To a purchaser wishing to restore this ancient relic, the advantage of raising building stone on the spot would be very great.'

In 1869, 'being in a very dilapidated state', it passed into the hands of T.B. Saunders of the Priory 'who proceeded to restore it, with great taste and judgment and at considerable expense' (figs. 40 and 41).[51] Before the restoration the interior was excavated to the depth of 10 feet below the floor. The chapel opened for worship in 1871. The east window was original apart from new mullions and repaired tracery. The other windows were designed 'from parts of the former window' found during the excavation. The niche on the south side of the east window was restored and the one on the north side apart from the haft and canopy was newly made to match the other. The cross over the east window was restored, the upper part having been found in the ruins. The new north

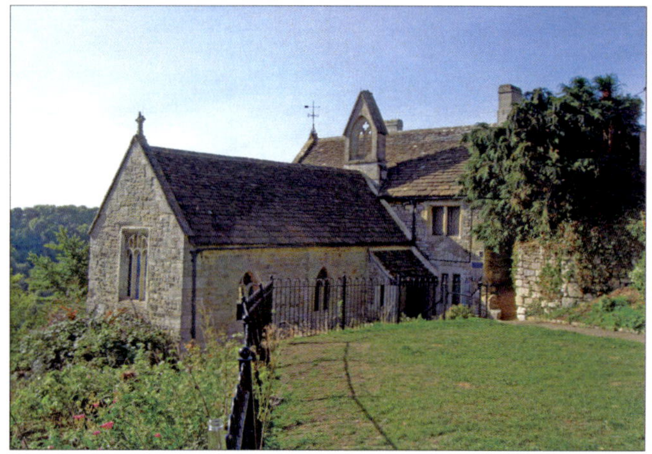

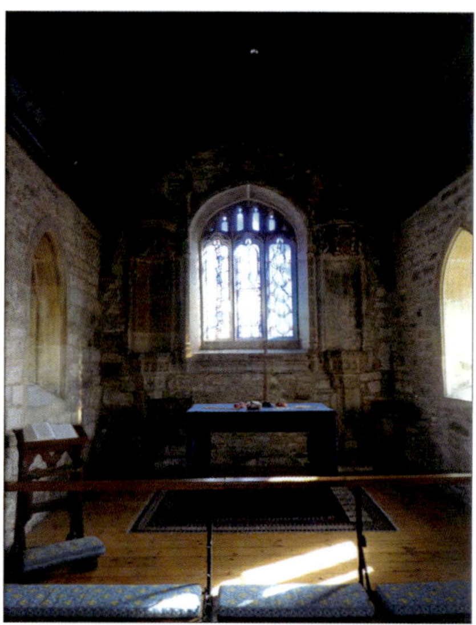

Above, Fig. 40: St Mary Tory

Above right, Fig 41: Interior of St. Mary Tory

porch included the holy water stoup found during the excavation (fig. 42). The chapel was renamed St. Mary's Chapel because of its position above Lady Well.

The *Pictorial Guide to Bradford-on-Avon* of 1887 says, 'There is a subterranean passage from the Hermitage' and this is repeated in Kelly's Directory with the unlikely suggestion that it led to the churchyard and Barton Farm. A map of 1887 (1:500 scale) shows paths where visitors could walk up to see the hermit cave half way up the quarry face and flights of steps continuing to the hilltop. Today there are two blocked quarry adits in the cliff face. The upper one has a doorway and a window carved out of the rock and there are three short tunnels at the back of the cave. On the east side of the plot there was another cave, the cellar of one of a pair of small houses which once stood there marked on Ashmead's map and the tithe map. This part of the site has recently been redeveloped.

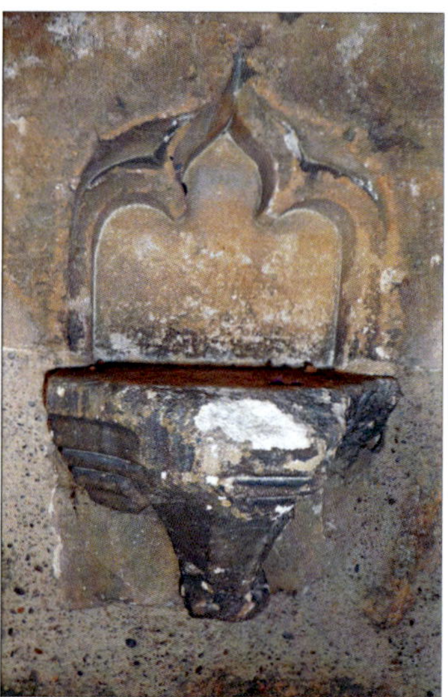

Fig. 42: Holy water stoup in the entrance porch

Budbury House, later the Rug Factory

A large building dominates the Budbury skyline from the town. During the 19th century rope making and allied industries were developed in Bradford. William Taylor was a rope maker in Church Street in 1822 and Edward Taylor was making rope and sacking in the mid-19th century. He built a Rope Walk on the south side of Newtown. He expanded his business into rug making and in about 1850 he built what was later called Budbury House on top of the hill as a rug factory (fig. 43). He also made tents, marquees and coconut matting. Called Wiltshire Rug Company's Works, it was still operating in 1939.[52] But Stephen Mizen was a private resident at Budbury House in 1890.

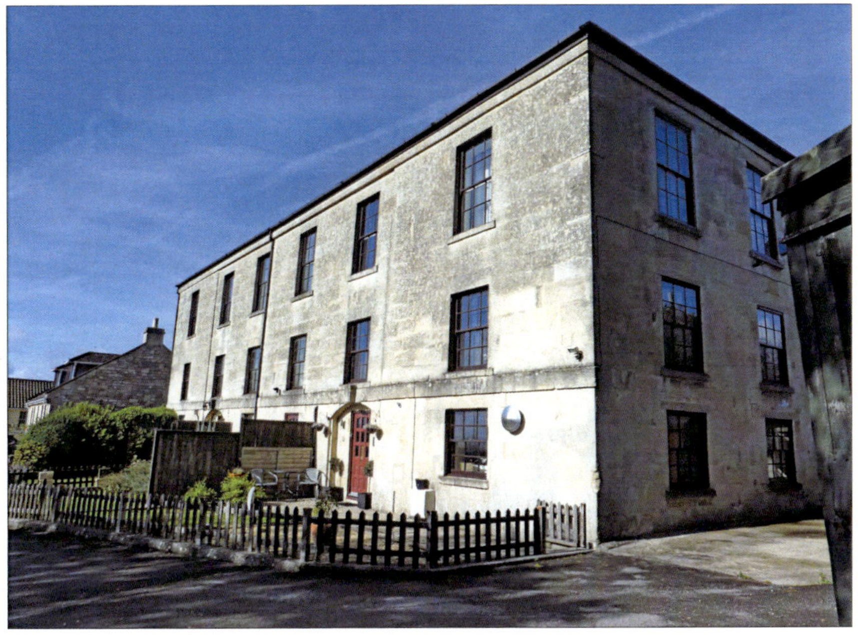

Fig. 43: Budbury House

Newtown Brewery

The former brewery in Newtown on the corner of Wine Street is a magnificent example of the local stone masons' craft. During the 18th century the Seven Stars Inn, now 19 Newtown, had a malthouse attached on the west side and a brewery behind. The Sandell family who ran it became allied by marriage with the Wilkins family. Alexander Wilkins moved the brewery operation over to the old quarry site below St. Mary Tory. He used the former England's cloth factory at the back of the site and added a new brewery building at the front (fig. 44). On the ground floor it had two parallel vaulted storage areas, two storeys tall with the brewing area above (figs. 45 and 46). There is a tunnel under Wine Street to move barrels to the inn.

In the period 1835-46 Henry Wilkins, brother of Alexander, used the adjoining part of the quarry site as a tanyard. In 1856-9 Alexander bought the tanyard from his brother and constructed a large malthouse (figs. 47-50). He retained a vaulted room on the ground floor and above this built a steeping area. To this he added long malting floors supported on iron pillars made at William Coles' foundry in Trowbridge Road with a malting kiln at the east end. Stables for dray horses were underneath. On all levels the builders had to cope with the uneven quarry face using vaulting or other techniques. It

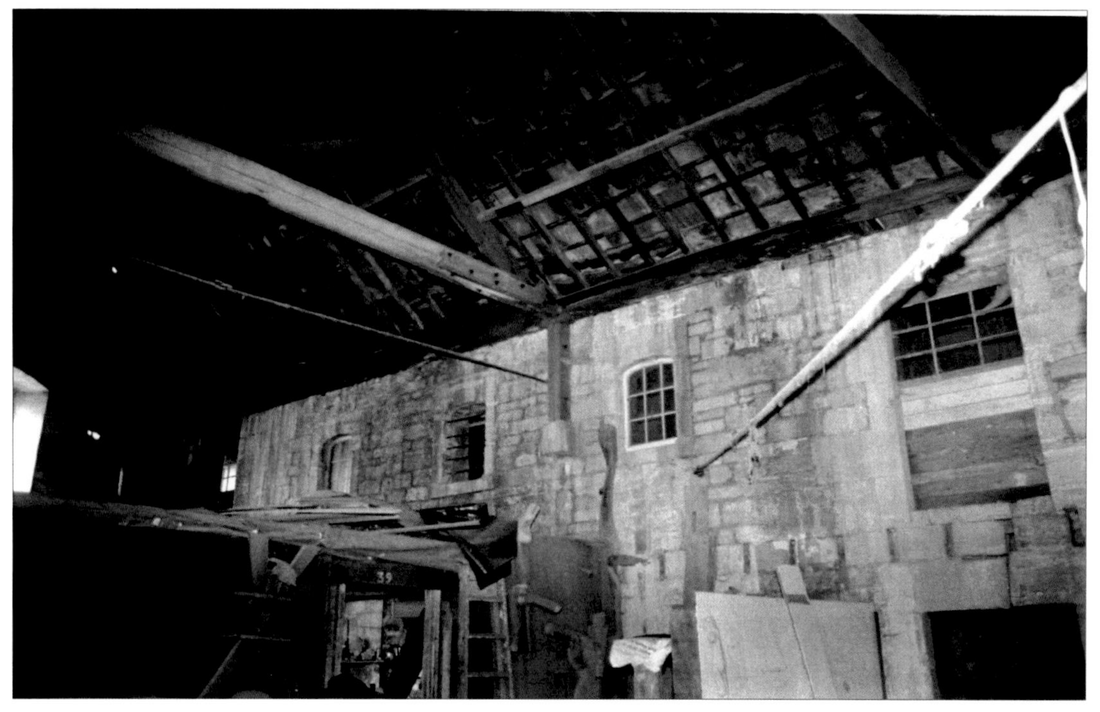

Fig. 44: South wall of the cloth workshop inside the brewery (WBR)

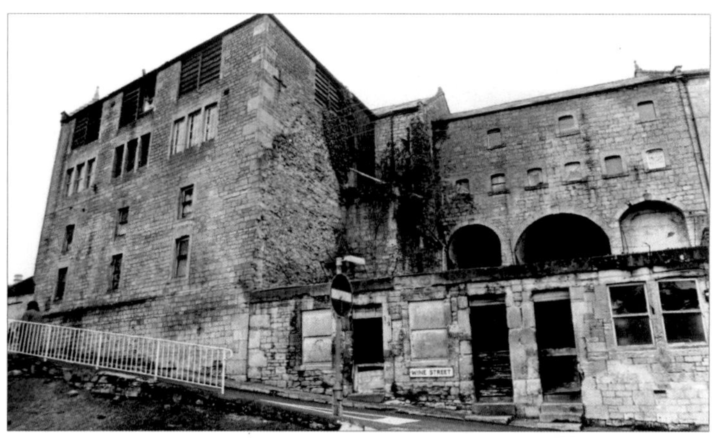

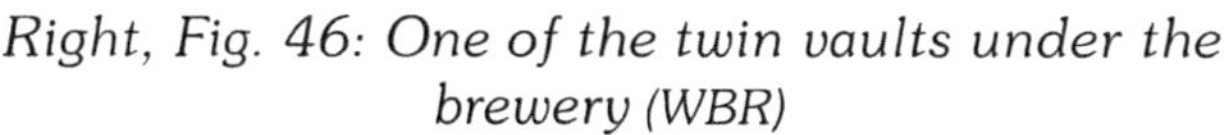

Above, Fig. 45: Newtown Brewery before conversion (WBR)

Right, Fig. 46: One of the twin vaults under the brewery (WBR)

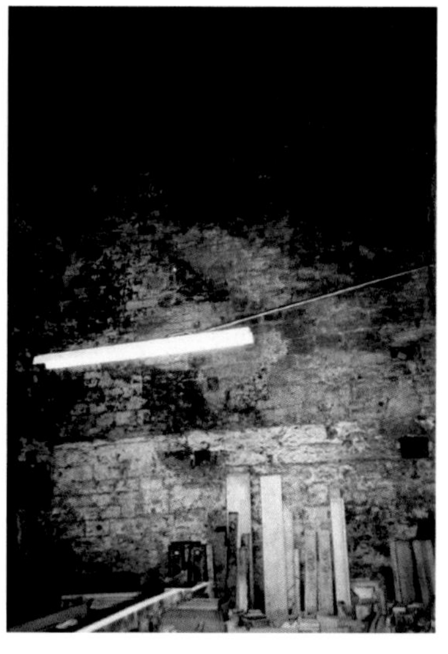

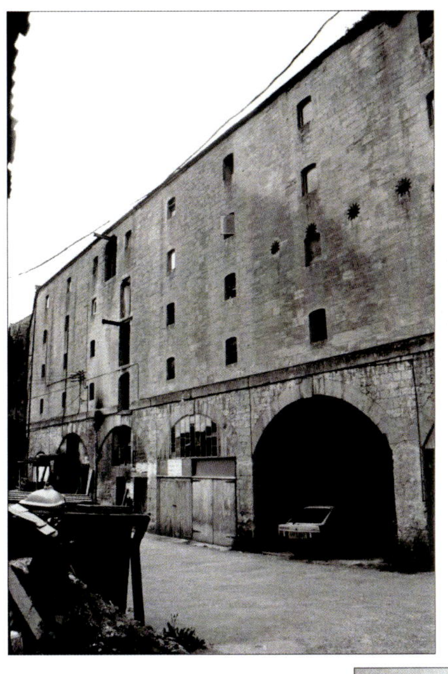

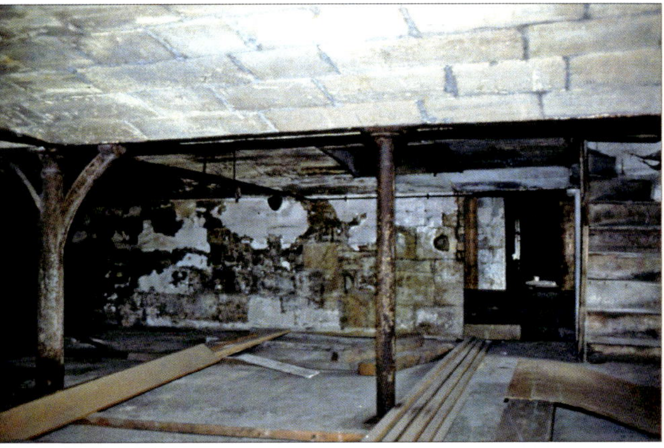

Left, Fig. 47: The malthouse before conversion (WBR)

Above, Fig. 48: Malting floor with iron pillars and stone ceiling (WBR)

Right, Fig 49: Ashmead's map of 1837 showing the brewery, the adjoining quarry and Ladywell cottages

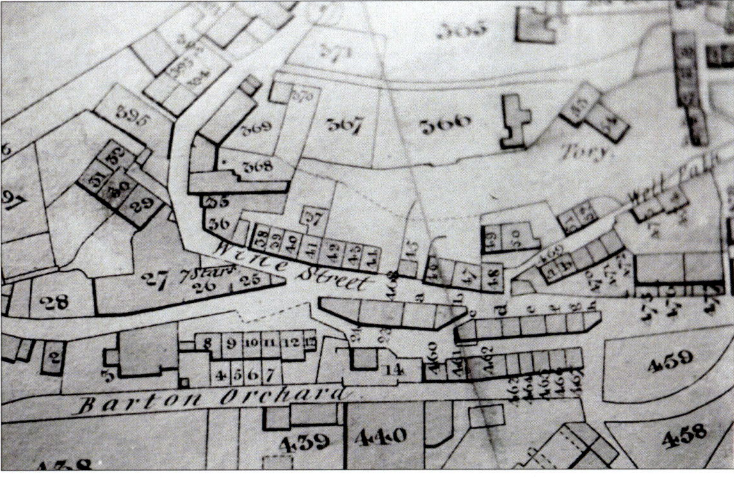

Below, Fig. 50: Ashmead's map of 1864 with the malthouse added and cottages removed

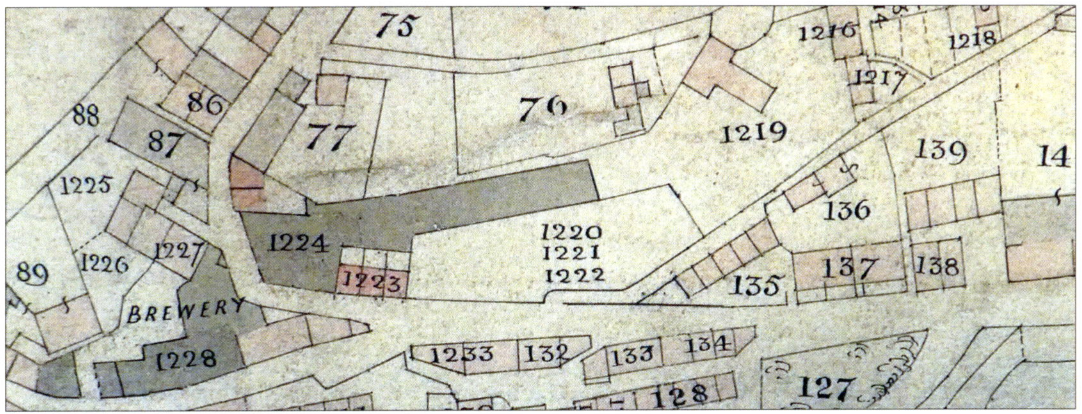

was funded by a mortgage of £900.

The spring water of Lady Well supplied the brewery and a cistern was built under the yard. From about 1860 the stream also fed the Newtown Spout with its horse trough and powered an underground iron water wheel (still extant) 18 feet in diameter. A Town Sewers plan of 1876 suggests the water wheel was used to power chaff-cutting for the dray horses. When the Public Baths in Bridge Street opened in 1898, it was supplied with water from Ladywell. A pipe was taken along the bed of the Avon and still carries water seen bubbling up near Westbury Gardens.

Wellpath

The two old routes climbing Budbury hill were Wellpath from Barton Farm and Conigre Hill from the town. A stone viaduct now carries Well Path over the entrance door to the plot with Ladywell spring (fig. 51a and b). This odd arrangement is explained by events

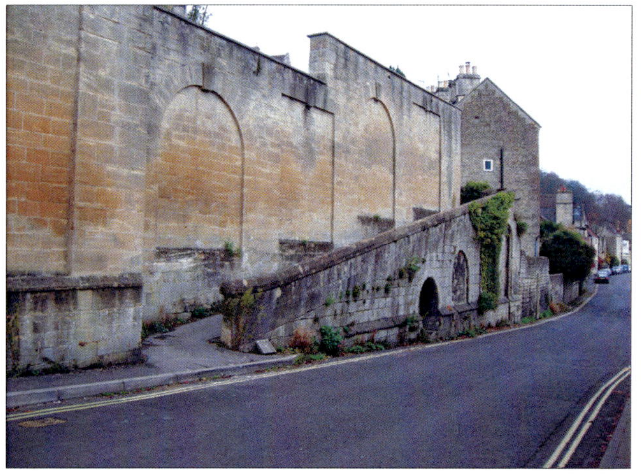

Fig. 51a: Wellpath and Ladywell horse trough

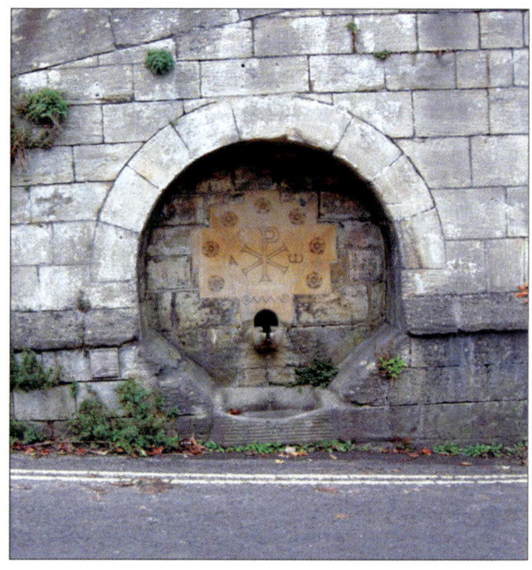

Fig. 51b: Horse trough with decoration designed by M. Valatin

in the mid-19th century. The building of the new front wall of Alexander Wilkins' brewery cut off access to the bottom of Wellpath. On 29th August 1856 the Town Commissioners ordered that it should be reinstated. Wilkins, who was himself Chairman of the Town Commissioners, provided stone for the work from his quarry apart from the ashlar facing stones and in October a tender from the builder Richard Newman was accepted.

This was not the end of the matter. Alexander Wilkins died in 1861. It was claimed in Bradford Magistrates' Court in December 1862 that the plan had taken land from T. B. Saunders and he had now been given it back by the Commissioners with permission to replace Wellpath.[53] Saunders employed the builder Charles Long to carry this out but when he was working there with two labourers, Thomas Jones and James Bricker, H. S. Wilkins, son of Alexander, arrived with Henry Jones and ordered him to stop work. He came back later with another man called Hillman and threatened to take their tools away. He returned again with four men, William Morris, Thomas Morris, George Moore and James Whistler. In trying to take the pickaxe off Thomas Jones, Thomas Morris fell into the hole they had excavated. A fight ensued. Charles Long said that the springhead was about 15 feet inside the brewery premises and flowed into Mr Saunders' old reservoir. He was making a 'passage for water'. He said Wilkins had rebuilt an old wall three feet further over encroaching on Wellpath. He found the foundations of the old footpath when he was digging. The magistrates decided they had no jurisdiction over titles to land and hoped for some arrangement between the parties. So the wall of the brewery is now stepped in to allow for the Wellpath viaduct over the Ladywell plot. The involvement of Henry Jones suggests it may have been the Jones family who built the brewery.

Newtown tollhouse

Another alteration in this cramped area came when the Newtown tollhouse was removed by the Town Commissioners to widen the road.[54] Newtown was turnpiked as part of an improved route from the top of Market Street to Winsley and on to Bath. This replaced the steep and tortuous Wine Street with a widened and in places realigned road through Belcombe to Turleigh, constructed in about 1819-20. The toll house at the Newtown bar was owned in 1820 by the lord of the manor Benjamin Hobhouse and the tenant was E. Williams, probably the shoemaker Ephraim Williams. Its tiny plot opposite Barton Steps was plot 137 on the tithe map. In 1839 the gate was repositioned to Turleigh. On 18th September 1862 it was minuted that Mr Saunders had given up his interest in the land by Wellpath as well as the interest of the representatives of the late Mr Bush in the Old Toll House in Newtown. He had handed over the key to the Commissioners. Mr A. Forster had also given up a portion of his land adjoining the toll house for the benefit of the town to effect the widening of the road. Bradford Turnpike Trust ceased operating altogether in 1872.[55] Despite this improvement the road by Barton Steps remains narrow to this day.

The search for a source of water for the town

In 1877 Bradford Town Commissioners investigated the possibility of providing a mains water supply for the town.[56] They looked first at Ladywell, still used by T.B. Saunders to supply the Priory and other houses. The Wilkins brothers would not say whether they would sell the springhead within the Newtown Brewery or charge a royalty on the water extracted. Canon Jones at the Vicarage and other house owners served by Ladywell threatened legal action as their supply would be affected.

After several sites at Avoncliff also fell through, the possibility of using the existing Budbury Well on top of the hill was explored. Temporary pumps were to be installed in spring 1880 to test the quality of its water and money borrowed from the Local Government Board to fund work. A tender was accepted for a pump capable of raising 18,000 gallons an hour from a depth of 140 feet and to pump for four weeks. The Local Government Board required a provisional agreement to purchase the well. A leading geologist, Mr Bristow, was convinced that there was in the area a large underground 'reservoir' of water separate from the springs supplying Ladywell. By mid June a shaft about 84 feet deep had been dug and from this an adit 100 feet long had been driven out. The geology of Budbury comprises Forest Marble under the surface (a hard stone suitable for tiles and paving stones) with Great Oolite limestone (a good building stone) below and Fuller's Earth clay below that.[57] The adit was above a layer of Fuller's Earth and they therefore expected the overlying strata to be impervious rock. They also put a trial borehole in the bottom of the well to find out the thickness of the underlying clay. When they did not find sufficient water, further long adits were driven out to the north and northeast at considerable expense and still to no avail. The scheme was abandoned in July 1880 and eventually another site at Avoncliff was used.

In 1881 Saunders claimed compensation for the work at Budbury. The wall inside the well needed repair, the well house needed repaving, the windlass re-fixing, the top of the well rebuilt and soil carted away. The commissioners claimed the well was worth £100 more than previously but they offered £50 compensation or to restore it. In the end Saunders settled for £75. A wellhouse is shown in the south-east corner of tithe award plot 21, The Park (fig. 52). During World War II it was used by neighbouring houses.[58]

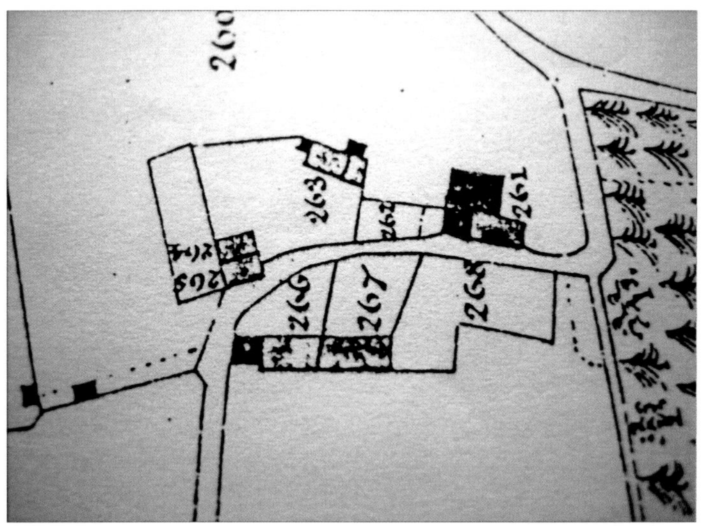

Fig. 52: Ashmead's map 1837, showing the path to Budbury Well

It was brick built and roofed. The infilled well is now under Budbury Close. There were other wells on top of the hill. One marked on the 1884 OS map was in front of no. 4 and another at that date was at Budbury Park Cottage. There is said to have been one which is now under the lock-up garages.[59] It is shown on the 1901 map behind a row of houses. There is also a well between the fish pond at Budbury Farm and the house next door.[60]

Changes to Newtown

The terrace of houses by Wellpath, 27-31 Newtown, was built by the carpenter and builder James Batten in 1820-1. He was the second son of Isaac Batten junior of Bearfield and took over his father's quarry there. His father lived at the junction of Huntingdon Street with Winsley Road.[61]

Some houses on the Budbury side of Newtown have still retained their original gabled appearance of the 1690s but some fronts were altered in the 18th century and more in the 19th century. The main alteration to no. 49 took place in 1827 when cabinet maker William Gough built forward onto the small front garden and upwards providing an extra storey (fig. 53). He constructed a cellar, perhaps as the family kitchen and probably used the ground floor front room as a showroom or shop with the rear room as his office. The family's living rooms were on the upper floors. The building remained a shop for a long time and was just one of the commercial premises along Newtown. There were three public houses there in 1822; The Bell at the east end, The Mason's Arms and the White Lion at no. 39 (fig. 54). [62] There were also several small shops. Nos. 40 and 41 have matching shop windows and no. 44 was also a shop (figs. 55). Nos. 47 and 48 Newtown were originally one house. The owners of 48 say that it was once owned by the Trustees of the Union Society (connected with the Zion Chapel). Leather and shoe-making items including bradawls and an iron shoe heel were found there.

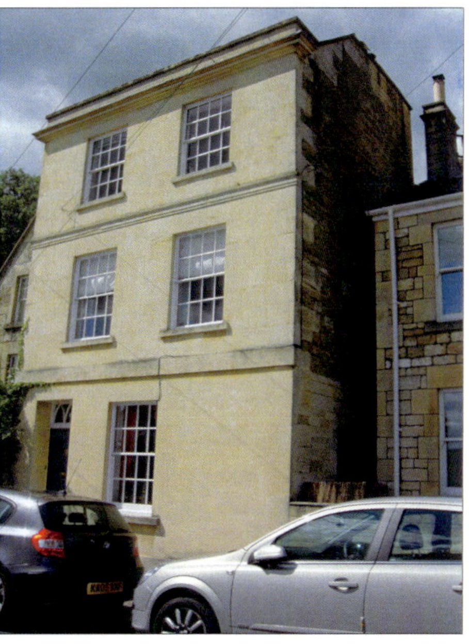

Fig. 53: 49 Newtown (WBR)

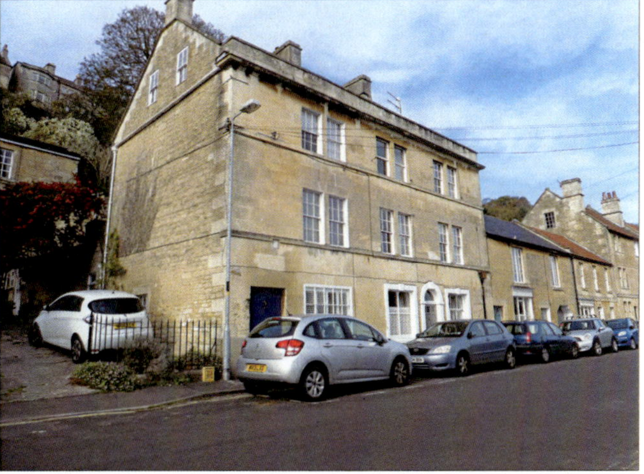

Fig. 54: Former White Lion, Newtown

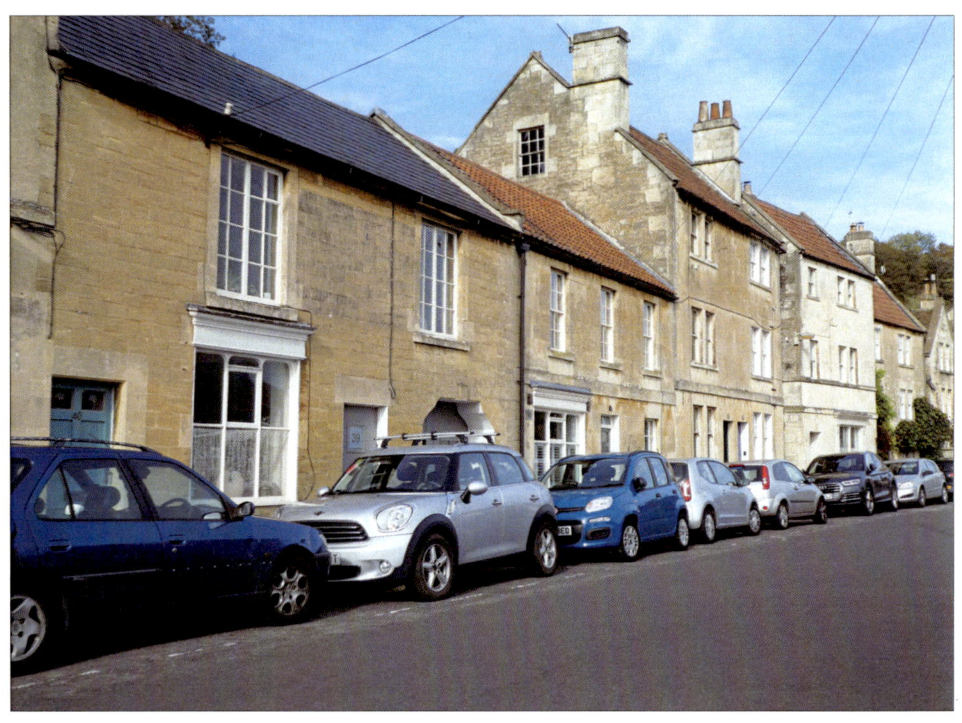

Fig.55: 40 and 41 Newtown with shop fronts

8 The Twentieth Century

Budbury Manor

The house was auctioned on December 13th 1928 as 15 and 16 Budbury Place and sold to Francis H. Wicks. He was the current tenant of both parts, now one 'cottage'. It had a walled-in garden and small poultry run. It still had an outside W.C. In 1915 Wick was described as a shopkeeper but at his death in 1940 he was described as a retired coachman.[1] After this his son Ted brought his family to live there and worked as Head Groundsman at the Winsley Sanitorium. He was a keen bell ringer at Holy Trinity Church. When his mother died in 1975 the house had been re-numbered as 4 Budbury Place. It was sold in 1977 to Ed Gilby who repaired and modernised it, returning the layout to a single house. He sold it in 1993 to the publisher, Roger Jones. The present owners are Peter and Jane Mann.

The farm buildings

The buildings of Budbury Barton, now 5 Budbury Place, were converted to an attractive house called Budbury Farm in 1925 for the Misses Pearson Godwin.[2] The architects were Rolfe & Peto of Bath; William Benjamin Rolfe (1872-1952) and Harold Peto, best known for his work on the gardens at Iford Manor. Peto trained with Edwin Lutyens in the architectural practice of Ernest George.[3] There are no drawings of the buildings before conversion but the existing fabric is distinguished by colour from the proposed alterations in the planning application.

After Miss Edith Anne Pearson died, on April 5th 1940, her possessions were assessed for probate by Quartley Son and White. They included paintings, fine furniture, silver and china. In 1948 plans were submitted and approved by Hugh Roberts & Davies of Bath to convert part of the buildings into a self-contained flat. A new dormer door entrance reached by outside steps matched the existing dormer windows. In 1953 Miss A.M.J.D. Godwin lived at 1 Budbury Place and as a separate household (probably in the flat O. H. Varga.[4]

The house was sold in 1956, still as Budbury Farm. As 1 Budbury Place, in about 1968, it was occupied by Frank Edward Flood, Secretary of Ushers Brewery. Mr and Mrs Colin Pearce, the present owners, came in 1983.

The hilltop

In 1938 an Observation Post of the Royal Observer Corps was set up at Budbury Ridge, east of Budbury Place on the far side of a field owned by Miss Godwin (of Budbury Farm) and later by Mr Flood.[5] This was part of an air raid warning system for the RAF. The panoramic view included the airfield at Keevil. The Corps was 'stood down' on May 10th 1945.

Guy Underwood, a retired solicitor, amateur archaeologist and Town Councillor, began excavating at Budbury in 1945. Despite his objections and raising £500 from the public to buy the land, ten prefabs were built at Budbury Circle and occupied by 1947.[6] Four were south-east of Winsley Road, north of the Budbury Circle road, two were south of the road and three more south-west of these last.

In the summer of 1969 when there was a plan to build a block of council flats at Budbury, an eight week excavation of the site on the east side of 54, Winsley Road, led by Geoffrey Wainwright, took place.[7] After this an estate of private houses was built. The architect Vernon Gibbs built a house for himself on the west side of the hill at 48 Budbury Close (fig. 56). Gradually housing is covering all the open areas of the hillfort.

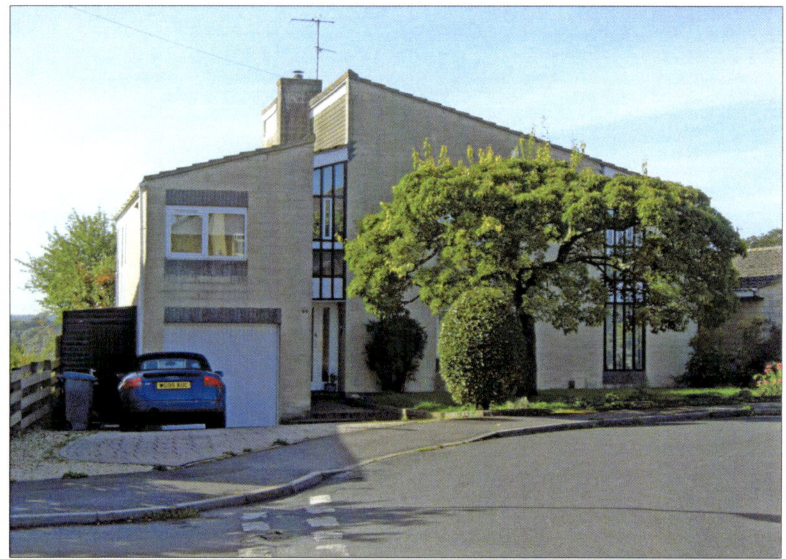

Fig. 56: 48 Budbury Close designed by Vernon Gibbs

Rug Factory

The Rug factory, formerly Budbury House, had closed by 1953. The building was later occupied by Fawt Engineering Vulcan Works. It was converted to housing as Budbury Court in 1981 with extensive alterations. Small houses on the north side of the factory had been pulled down (perhaps in the late 1960s) and UDC garages for the residents of Tory were built.[8]

Winsley Road and Bearfield

A number of new houses were built along Winsley Road in the 1930s in the typical ribbon development of the period. Budbury Tyning was built in 1954 on the north side of the road on the field of the same name which had been allotments.[9] Two other housing estates were built on the north side. The Churches estate of 42 council houses was built in the early 1950s on an area of former surface quarrying.[10] The Downs View estate of private houses was built from 1965 on the west side on land owned by Mr Butler.[11] G.N. Butler was farming at Grove Farm, Winsley Road in 1969.[12]

Bungalows were built west of Huntingdon Street in the 1960s on a paddock and allotments in a new road called Huntingdon Rise.[13] Church Acre off Huntington Street, an estate of semi-detached houses was built on former orchard and quarry land between Bearfield Buildings and Winsley Road from about 1965.

Newtown

This was still a busy commercial street in 1911.[14] On the north side between Wine Street and Conigre Hill there was first the Pickwick Brewery of Wilkins Bros & Hudson Ltd (now named after the owners' other brewery at Corsham). They were described as brewers and maltsters, wine and spirit merchants and, a current fashion, mineral water manufacturers. Other commercial enterprises were; no. 39 The former White Lion, now William Penny & Son, bakers and grocers, no. 41 James Moore, grocer, no. 44 Mark White, pork butcher, no. 47 Thomas Bigwood & Son, plumber, no. 49 Fanny Archard, shopkeeper, no. 52 Alfred Guy Mould, Masons' Arms, no. 53 Walter G. Collins, photographer and United Patriots' National Benefit Society, no. 62 Mrs Jane Ann Elliot, The Bell.

The century saw the decline and gradual removal of commerce from the street. The brewery was sold to Ushers of Trowbridge, probably in 1918, and by 1926 it was disused.[15] In 1946 Ushers sold the buildings to the Enfield Cycle Company Ltd. In 1955 they sold them to the builder Stanley H. Long, who was already using the premises as a yard and workshops. He was followed by his son Michael Berkeley Long. In 1990 the builders Berkeley Long and their tenants ceased using the site and in 1991, after its sale, a conversion into flats and offices began.

Demolitions and refurbishment in Wine Street and the hillside above Newtown

From the start of the century until the 1930s Tory, Middle Rank and especially Wine Street were all considered to be 'rough' areas of the town.[16] Children from other areas were afraid to pass that way when going to school. Cadby Place, the terrace of houses in Wine Street was demolished in 1958.[17] Run-down houses in Middle Rank and Tory were also threatened in the 1950s (fig. 57).[18] Nos. 1-10 Tory were compulsorily purchased and many of the families were relocated to the new Churches estate. In 1962-3 the houses were renovated with funds from various sources and then so were nos. 23 and 24 at the other end.[19] The better houses at the west end became sought after in the late 1930s. The end house near St Mary Tory was owned by Lady Bowes-Lyon as a summer holiday cottage.[20]

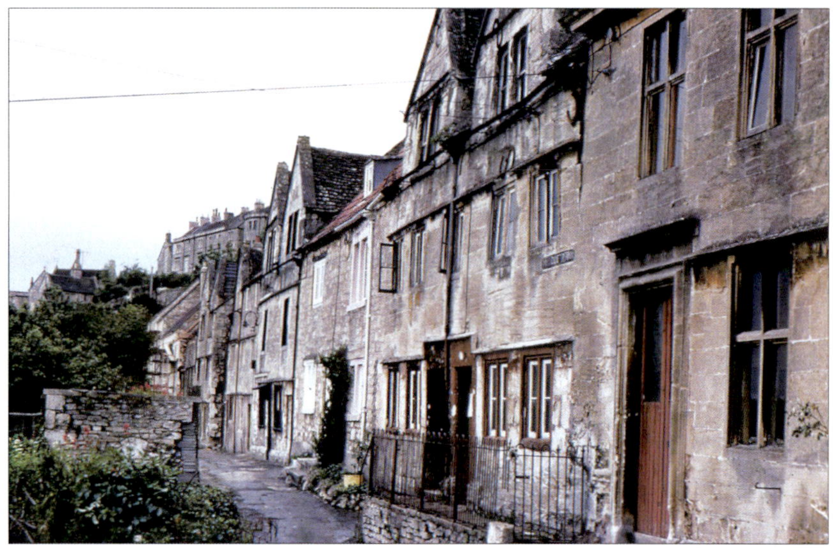

Fig. 57: Middle Rank before renovation (WCC)

Middle Rank was tackled in the 1960s. Part of the Rank was compulsorily purchased and rebuilt in facsimile. 4 Middle Rank was restored in 1978 through Town Scheme funding.[21] All the houses on the hillside when brought up to modern standards attracted new residents from the professional classes.

Conclusion

Centred originally on the Iron Age hill fort and the Roman villa, the Budbury area developed in the Middle Ages as a manor separate from Bradford. Its fortunes then became linked with the hamlet of Ashley, north of Winsley. At the end of the 17th century the busy industrial borough of Bradford began to encroach on the open hillside with the building of the three ranks of housing which now provide the backdrop to the town. To the north, Huntingdon Street and Bearfield Buildings developed as a separate community housing cloth workers and quarrymen. In the 19th century a scattering of small houses was built in Wine Street and on top of the hill. Newtown became a commercial street with the brewery, malthouse, public houses and shops. Finally the hilltop and all the surrounding areas were infilled with housing in the 20th century.

But a degree of separateness persisted. Most of the area, for example, was not brought under the control of the new Bradford Town Commissioners in 1839. In the 1980s when Margaret Dobson interviewed local people, those who lived 'on top of the hill' felt quite separate from the people who lived in the lower part of the town or across the river. They still enjoyed their own shops, places of worship and events.[22] Today the area feels more completely incorporated within the town and, to most people, 'Budbury' signifies simply a small modern estate off the Winsley Road.

Acknowledgements

We are grateful to Peter Mann, Roger Mawby, Margaret Dobson and Roger Clark for additional historical information and to Robert Arkell for maps. Also to Roger Jones of Ex Libris Press for design and typesetting.

Orton Jewellery, Market Street, Bradford-on-Avon,

has provided generous sponsorship of this publication.

Illustrations

By the authors except where stated. BL British Library, WBR Wiltshire Buildings Record, WCC Wiltshire County Council, WSA Wiltshire and Swindon Archives

Notes and references

Introduction
1   R. and B. Harvey, *Winsley*, 54

1 The Archaeology of Budbury
1   R. Canham: *A Land through Time*, Bradford on Avon Museum 2014
2   Wiltshire Historic Environment Record ST76SE607
3   W. H. Jones: *An Account of the Parish of Bradford-on-Avon*, 1859
4   G. Wainwright 'An Iron Age promontory fort at Budbury, Bradford-on-Avon, Wiltshire' *WANHM* 65, 108-166
5   M. and H. Whittock: *Anglo-Saxon Bradford-on-Avon*, Bradford-on-Avon Museum Monograph No. 1
6   *WANHM* 65, 120-1
7   *WANHM* 112, forthcoming
8   *Bulletin of the Association for Roman Archaeology*, Issue 16, March 2004
9   *WANHM 112*, forthcoming

2 The Medieval Period
1   SANHS vol.144, 119
2   E. Ekwall: *English Place-names*, 72, Mawer & Stenton: *The Place-names of Wiltshire*, 117
3   J. MacDonald: *Monarchs, Murder, Mystery and Mayhem*, 2000, 26
4   *VCH* vol. 7, 13, *WANHM* vol. 91 (1998), 80
5   N.E. Stacy (ed), *Charters and Custumals of Shaftesbury Abbey 1089-1216*, 2006, 37
6   R. Harvey, 'Shaftesbury Abbey's 12th century Rentals for Bradford-on-Avon' *WANHM* vol. 91 (198). He was probably named after the village of Coulston, Wilts
7   R. Harvey, *WANHM* vol. 91 (1998), 76-89
8   R. & B. Harvey: *Winsley, from Cecilia to Victoria*, 2007, 31
9   Stacy, 201
10 Stacy, 204
11 Stacy, 55-6
12 VCH vol. 7, 16 and 42
13 WRS vol. 65, 40
14 R. B. Harvey and B. K. Harvey 'Bradford-on-Avon in the 14th Century', *WANHM* vol. 86 (1993), 128

15 WRS vol. 33, 60
16 WRS vol. 1, 49
17 VCH vol. 7, 16
18 WRS vol. 45, 121

3 Budbury manor is joined with Ashley manor
1   R. And B. Harvey: *Winsley*, 31
2   Harvey: 41
3   WRS, vol.45, 121
4   WRS, vol.29, 109
5   Per P. Mann
6   WRS, vol.42, 45
7   Harvey: 40
8   Website dedicated to the genealogy of the Ashley-Cooper family. K. H. Rogers: *Book of Trowbridge*, (1984), 27
9   K. H. Rogers: *Medieval Trowbridge*, (2016), 23
10 Rogers: *Medieval Trowbridge*, 23
11 Website History of Parliament
12 WRS: vol.60, 11-12
13 WRS: vol.60, 75-76, 84
14 WRS: vol.42, 87
15 WRS: vol. 60, 84
16 Website
17 Harvey: 41

4 The Sixteenth Century
1   Harvey: *Winsley*, 51
2   WSA P2/3Reg/16B
3   WSA P2/5Reg/151A
4   The estate of James Pickering, husbandman of Woolley, Bradford was administered in 1603, WSA P2/P/144
5   WSA 212B/522 and a fuller version WSA 1742/3245
6   British Library Egerton Ms. 36543
7   WSA P2/7Reg/79D
8   WSA 1742/1999

5 The Seventeenth Century
1   British Library Egerton 3652/112-114 Note of all the burgages, c.1600
2   Calendar of Patent Rolls, Gaol Delivery
3   WSA 1742/4584
4   WSA 1742/4576
5   WSA 1742/4579
6   WSA 1742/3244

7   TNA Prob/11/118
8   WSA 947/
9   WSA P2/5Reg/6B
10 WSA 1742/
11 Bathampton Local History Research Group Bathampton Down, 2017
12 WSA 2845/4
13 *WANHM* vol. 19, 255
14 WSA 1742/3246
15 WSA 1742/4592
16 Holt registers
17 WSA 1742/4577
18 WSA 1742/4581
19 WSA 212B/514
20 Harvey: *Winsley*, 143
21 Aubrey's *Natural History of Wiltshire* Part 2, Chap.11
22 K. Rogers: *The Domestic Woollen Industry at Bradford-on-Avon* (2014); Aubrey & Jackson Wiltshire Collections, 21
23 WSA 1742/3268
24 Information from Roger Mawby. It was called just Bearfield Farm in the 19th century.
25 WSA 1742/6400 and typed copy 1742/6401
26 WANHM 32, 401
27 WSA 1742/3297
28 Aubrey & Jackson Wiltshire Collections, 21
29 Aubrey's Natural History, 56
30 WSA 1742/2257
31 Will of John Skrine, owner of the house adjoining to the west, WSA P2/S/1374
32 WSA A1/250
33 WSA 1742/2260

6   The Eighteenth Century

1   WSA 1742/6785 with thanks to Roger Mawby for this and some of the following records
2   WSA P2/S/1224 and P1/S/967
3   WANHM vol. 32, 402
4   WSA 1742/3263
5   M. J. Slocombe, Clothiers to Gentlemen, MA thesis, Sussex University
6   Thomas Methuen's portrait reproduced in R. F. Carr Storied Urns, (1998), 65
7   WSA 1742/
8   WSA P2/D/660
9   WSA P1/D/424 and P1/14Reg/31
10 Guardian Angel Issue No. 62
11 Bodleian Library MS.Top.Wilts.c.2, fol.29

12 R. and B. Harvey: History of Abbey House, Bradford-on-Avon, Wilts. Buildings Record
13 WANHM 69 (1974), 166
14 Carr: *Storied Urns*, 30-31
15 R. and B. Harvey, history of Abbey House, WBR.
16 Info. R. Mawby
17 Harvey: *Winsley*
18 WSA 947/1334 deed of partition
19 VCH, vol. 7, 8
20 VCH, vol. 7, 41
21 Info. R. Mawby
22 P. M. Slocombe: *Architects and Building Craftsmen with Work in Wiltshire* Part 2, (2006), 115
23 WSA Wilkins & Hill collection, Box 6741, Box 6476 B
24 WSA 206/5a
25 WSA Wilkins & Hill, Box 6746
26 WSA 947/1331
27 WSA 1742/
28 WSA 1742/4617
29 WSA 1890/Box 6736 F
30 Rebuilt on old cellars in 1891.
31 Info. R. Mawby

7   The Nineteenth Century

1   Church Rate Book, W.T. 77-2
2   Poor Rate Book
3   Info. R. Mawby
4   Deeds seen by Bradford-on-Avon Museum
5   M. Dobson and G. Slater: *Barton Farm – The Last Thousand Years*, (2016)
6   WRS, vol. 47
7   This is the first deed with the present owners
8   Town directory
9   *Bath Chronicle* 4.3.1813
10 Tithe Award
11 Census 1841
12 J. Mock *Bradford's Pubs and Breweries*, (2012), 51
13 P. Slocombe: *Architects and Building Craftsmen with Work in Wiltshire* Part 2
14 *Wiltshire Independent*, 10th and 17th August 1843
15 *Devizes Advertiser* 21.3.1867
16 WRS Early Trade Directories, vol. 47
17 Slater's Directory
18 WSA 1742
19 Info. Roger Mawby
20 WRS vol.47, 64

21 Info. R. Mawby
22 M. Ashton and R. Mawby: 'Bradford's Castle Folly', *Guardian Angel* No. 35, Summer 2001
23 WRS vol. 47
24 G. Langdon: *Year of the Map*, 1976
25 Kelly's Directory
26 Ashton and Mawby Bradford's Castle Folly
27 O.S. map
28 B.S. Niblett Memories of Bradford-on-Avon
29 Info. Roger Clarke.
30 Niblett, 71
31 Jones: *The Parish of Bradford-on-Avon*, 8
32 Recorded by Adrian Powell.
33 Ashton and Mawby: *Bradford's Castle Folly*. It is also named on Ashmead's map of 1837.
34 *News Chronicle*, 17.1.1939
35 British Library Skinner collection
36 Turnpike records
37 *Wiltshire Times* 4.11.1882
38 WSA G13/1/3
39 H. Fassnidge *Bradford on Avon Past and Present*, 56
40 WRS vol. 40, 96
41 WSA 1742
42 WSA 1742
43 WRS vol. 40, 96
44 WSA 1742
45 M. Dobson: *Bradford Voices*, 173
46 *Bath Chronicle*
47 WSA G13/990/42
48 Tithe Award
49 He later moved to Guernsey and the drawings are in Guernsey Museum. Copies in Wiltshire Buildings Record.
50 WSA poster
51 Kelly 1889
52 West Wilts Directory
53 *Trowbridge and North Wilts Advertiser*, 20 December 1862
54 WSA G13/1/2
55 WSA G13/1/3
56 WSA G13/1/5
57 I. Geddes: *Geology, Landscape and Building Stone around Bradford-on-Avon*, Bradford-on-Avon Museum
58 Info. Peter Mann quoting David Wicks
59 Info. Colin Pearce
60 Info. Colin Pearce
61 Info. R. Mawby
62 WRS 47

8 The Twentieth Century

1 Kelly's Directory
2 WSA G13/760/162
3 Photographs of the house after conversion, British Architectural Library.
4 WSA G13/760/403
5 *Bradford Voices*, 126-129
6 *Bradford Voices*, 149
7 The finds are at Wiltshire Museum, Devizes.
8 *Bradford Voices*, 198
9 *Bradford Voices*, 150
10 Niblett: *Memories of Bradford-on-Avon*, 71
11 *Bradford Voices*, 189
12 Bradford Directory
13 *Bradford Voices*, 83
14 Kelly's Directory
15 O.S. map
16 *Bradford Voices*, 91-93, 'You had to be a tough boy, just because if you didn't live there you'd get a hiding. If you walked along the top of Tory and Middle Rank you got a hiding; if you walked down Wine Street you got a hiding'.
17 *Bradford Voices*, 159
18 *Bradford Voices*, 161
19 *Bradford Voices*, 163-165
20 *Bradford Voices*, 93
21 *Bradford Voices*, 184
22 *Bradford Voices*, 89

More publications from Bradford-on-Avon Museum

- *The Christopher Pharmacy*
  by Ivor Slocombe & Roger Clark; *A5;* 14 pages; full colour; Price £2.00
- *Lost Pubs of Bradford on Avon: A Walker's Guide* by Roger Clark;
  A5; 12 pages; full colour; Price £2.50
- *Abbey Mill* by David Gazard
  A5; 16 pages; full colour; Price £3.00
- *Bradford-on-Avon Printers and Town Directories*
  by Roger Jones; A5; 28 pages; Price £2.50
- *The Saxon Church* by David A. Hinton
  A5; 24 pages; full colour; Price £2.50
- *The Hall, Bradford-on-Avon* by Pamela M. Slocombe
  Large format; 44 pages; full colour; Price £4.00
- *The Bridges of Bradford-on-Avon* by Ivor Slocombe
  A5; 28 pages; full colour; Price £3.00
- *A Land through Time* by Roy Canham
  A5; 24 pages; full colour; Price £3.00
- *The Woollen Industry at Bradford-on-Avon* by Kenneth Rogers
  A5; 24 pages; full colour; Price £3.00
- *Geology, Landscape and Building Stone around Bradford-on-Avon*
  by Isobel Geddes; A5; 28 pages; Price £3.00
- *The Buildings of Barton Farm, Bradford-on-Avon*
  by Pamela M. Slocombe and Ivor Slocombe
  Large format; 48 pages; full colour; Price £4.00
- *The Iron Duke: The machine that founded Bradford-on-Avon's rubber industry*
  by Roger Clark. 8 pages; full colour; Price £1.00
- *Riding on Rubber: The Story of Bradford-on-Avon's world-renowned Rubber
  Industry* by Dan Farrell. Large format; 112 pages; Price £9.75
- *Bradford Leigh Fair: 200 Years of Trade, Revelry, Wickedness and Vice*
  by Robert Arkell. A5; 44 pages; Price £4.00

Bradford-on-Avon Museum monographs ~

- *Anglo-Saxon Bradford-on-Avon* by Martin Whittock and Hannah Whittock
  A5; 28 pages; Price £3.00
- *Bradford-on-Avon: the Medieval Town* by Ivor & Pamela Slocombe
  A5; 32 Pages; Price £3.00